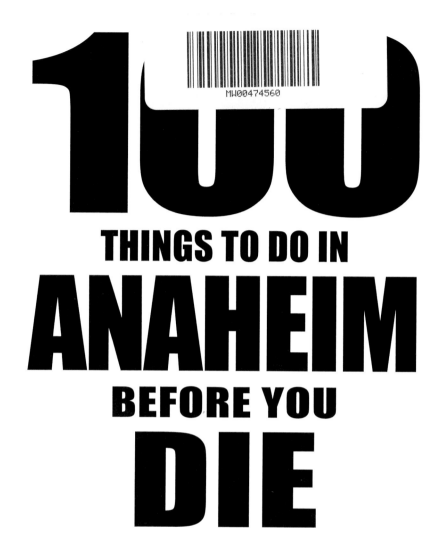

100
THINGS TO DO IN
ANAHEIM
BEFORE YOU
DIE

MW00474560

Founders' Park

100

THINGS TO DO IN

ANAHEIM

BEFORE YOU

DIE

• •

MELANIE WALSH

REEDY PRESS

Copyright © 2023 by Reedy Press, LLC
Reedy Press
PO Box 5131
St. Louis, MO 63139, USA
www.reedypress.com

No part of this publication may be reproduced or transmitted in any form or by any means, electronic or mechanical, including photocopy, recording, or any information storage and retrieval system, without permission in writing from the publisher.

Permissions may be sought directly from Reedy Press at the above mailing address or via our website at www.reedypress.com.

Library of Congress Control Number: 2023938646

ISBN: 9781681064505

Design by Jill Halpin

All images by the author unless otherwise noted.

Printed in the United States of America
23 24 25 26 27   5 4 3 2 1

We (the publisher and the author) have done our best to provide the most accurate information available when this book was completed. However, we make no warranty, guarantee, or promise about the accuracy, completeness, or currency of the information provided, and we expressly disclaim all warranties, express or implied. Please note that attractions, company names, addresses, websites, and phone numbers are subject to change or closure, and this is outside of our control. We are not responsible for any loss, damage, injury, or inconvenience that may occur due to the use of this book. When exploring new destinations, please do your homework before you go. You are responsible for your own safety and health when using this book.

DEDICATION

To Matt, Georgia, Harper, Poppy, and Mabel,
who make every day more magical.

CONTENTS

Preface xii

Acknowledgments xv

Food and Drink

1. Set Sail for Strong Water.. 2

2. Immerse Yourself in a Video Game at Requiem Cafe 3

3. Unpack New Flavors in the Anaheim Packing District......... 4

4. Tap the La Palma Beer Trail 6

5. Elevate Your Evening at The FIFTH 8

6. Feed Your Soul Chicken and Waffles at Roscoe's............... 9

7. Raise a Glass at Colony Wine Merchant 10

8. Start Your Day with a Salt & Butter Roll at Okayama Kobo
   Cafe & Bakery.. 11

9. Visit a Cantina Far, Far Away at Oga's Cantina 12

10. Order Salmon Chocolat at the Anaheim White House 13

11. Flip over the Original Pancake House 14

12. Meat Up at Windsor Brown's.. 15

13. Brighten Your Brews at Radiant Beer Co......................... 16

14. Chow Down on the MAC Daddy of Burgers at Craft
    by Smoke and Fire 17

• •

15. Grab a Joe Latti at Joe's Italian Ice **18**

16. Order a Brussel Sprout Taco at Pour Vida Tortillas and Taps **20**

17. Treat Yourself at House of Chimney Cakes **21**

18. Swirl Spaghetti at Mama Cozza's **22**

19. Reserve Your Seat at the Chef's Counter at Napa Rose **23**

20. Snag a Slice from Focaccia Boi **24**

21. Give 'Em Something to Taco 'Bout **26**

22. Brew the Blues at Sunbliss Cafe **28**

23. Drink Lebanese Wine at Rosine's **29**

24. Speak Easy at The Blind Rabbit **30**

25. Taste the Twist of Don Churro Gomez **31**

26. Gimme Sugar at Ralph Brennan's Jazz Kitchen **32**

27. Shake It Up at Black Tap Craft Burgers & Beers **34**

28. Say "OMG!" at OMG Dessert Lounge **35**

Music and Entertainment

29. Maximize the Magic at the Disneyland Resort **38**

30. Honor the Berry That Started It All at Knott's Berry Farm **40**

31. Float On Down for the Anaheim Halloween Parade **42**

32. Eat a Deep-Fried Oreo at the OC Fair **43**

33. Rock Out at the House of Blues Anaheim **44**

34. Get an Autograph at WonderCon **45**

• •

35. Two-Step at The RANCH Saloon.. 46

36. Catch a Broadway Show at the Segerstrom.. 47

37. Pick Your Dinner at Tanaka Farms... 48

38. Swashbuckle Your Way to Pirate's Dinner Adventure.......................... 49

39. Soar above the OC on the Great Park Balloon 50

40. Take Your Seat at Chance Theater... 51

41. Capture the Magic of Disney on Ice 52

42. See the Stars at City National Grove of Anaheim 53

43. Pop Over to Bubblefest at Discovery Cube 54

44. Craft a Great Night at Craft & Arts 55

45. Enter the Fog at Knott's Scary Farm 56

46. Get on the Nice List at the Grand Californian Hotel & Spa.................. 58

47. Spring Over to The Flower Fields... 59

Sports and Recreation

48. Play like Kobe at the Kobe Bryant Memorial Dream Court................. 62

49. Go on Strike at Splitsville 63

50. Chill Out at Anaheim Ice 64

51. Make It a Homerun Visit at Angel Stadium 65

52. Grind and Slide at Anaheim West Skatepark 66

53. Take a Hike at Oak Canyon Nature Center... 67

• •

54. Fly to the Honda Center **68**

55. Wipeout at the Adventure Lagoon **69**

56. Hit a Hole in One at the Anaheim Hills Golf Course **70**

57. Float Down the Lazy River at Soak City **71**

58. Take Over the Track at K1 Speed **72**

59. Catch a Wave in Huntington Beach **73**

60. Level Up at Arcade Mission Control **74**

61. Tweet about the Birds You See at Anaheim Coves **75**

62. Splish Splash in Anaheim Hotel Water Parks **76**

63. Have a Howlin' Good Time at Great Wolf Lodge **78**

64. Tackle the Trails at the Fullerton Loop **80**

65. Become a Beach Buccaneer at Pirate's Tower **81**

66. Channel Your Inner Maverick at Flightdeck **82**

67. Run Away to the Circus at SwingIt Trapeze **83**

68. Hit the Target at Sauced BBQ & Spirits **84**

69. Rent a Surrey at Irvine Regional Park **85**

Culture and History

70. Explore Little Arabia **88**

71. Sign Your John Hancock at Independence Hall **89**

72. Explore Anaheim's History at Founders' Park **90**

• •

73. Imagine Yourself in the Birthplace of Imagineering.............................. 92

74. Take In the Arts at Muzeo... 93

75. Say "Opa!" at the OC Greek Fest 94

76. Walk in Walt's Footsteps in His Disneyland Apartment 95

77. Put On Your Lederhosen for Oktoberfest 96

78. Explore the Evidence at the Richard Nixon Presidential
Library & Museum 98

79. Learn Guitar History at the Leo Fender Gallery 99

80. Take a Tour of Anaheim Art...100

81. Watch Art Come to Life at Pageant of the Masters 102

82. Visit LA's Historic Olvera Street 104

83. Await the Return of the Swallows at Mission San Juan Capistrano......106

84. Celebrate Unity at the Black History Month Parade 107

Shopping and Fashion

85. Get Hoppy at Windsor Home Brew Supply 110

86. Pick Up Pixie Dust at the World of Disney 111

87. Shop Vintage Fashion at RARE by Goodwill 112

88. Add Luxury to Your Bag at South Coast Plaza....................................114

89. Go Green at Eco Now 115

90. Save at the Outlets at Orange 116

• •

91. Build an Epic Charcuterie Board at Cortina's Italian Market **118**

92. Grab a Gift at SEED People's Market **119**

93. Shop Fresh at the Downtown Anaheim Farmers Market **120**

94. Build Your LEGO Collection at Bricks and Minifigs **121**

95. Unearth a Hidden Gem at Anaheim GardenWalk **122**

96. Find the Unconventional at The Lab **123**

97. Grab Anaheim Swag at Thank You Coffee **124**

98. Get Drop Dead Gorgeous Decor at Roger's Gardens **125**

99. Score at The Source **126**

100. Bring Home Blooms from Visser's Florist & Greenhouse **127**

Activities by Season **129**

Suggested Itineraries **133**

Index **135**

PREFACE

It wouldn't be much of a stretch to say I've been researching this book my entire life. As a fourth-generation Anaheim resident, I have filled my days and photo albums with highlights from around the city. While it's the largest in Orange County, Anaheim very much feels like a small town to me.

Growing up, my parents' garage served as our community's polling place. Election season felt like a celebration, with neighbors lined up in the driveway and my father sitting behind the registration table. It ignited a love for my community, one that I'm happily passing along to my four children.

With my husband and our daughters, I've gobbled up traditions at Anaheim's legacy restaurants like Mama Cozza's and sipped on new favorites at newcomers like Requiem Cafe in the name of research for this book. There have been thrills and sprinklings of pixie dust at local theme parks. There have been shopping sprees in malls and small businesses. It's a rough life, I tell you. If you don't believe me, I have chronicled our adventures on ClementineCounty.com for you to peruse.

Expanding to write *100 Things to Do in Anaheim Before You Die* has been a bucket list item of my own. I wanted to ensure locals like myself had a list of places in and around Anaheim to inspire their weekends and staycations. With Disneyland

and the Anaheim Convention Center drawing global visitors, I similarly hope this book serves as a guide to the most popular but also the unexpected.

Anaheim is magic, and I'm honored to share it with you.

Love mural

ACKNOWLEDGMENTS

To my husband and children, I owe you a million thank yous. Thank you for every adventure, every photo, and every taste test. I love sharing our "little" city with the world and wouldn't want to explore with anyone else but you.

Thank you also to my parents, Susan and Basil, who taught me what it means to be a part of a community.

Speaking of community, my neighbors welcomed us in and have become the greatest part of Anaheim.

A special shout-out to the team at Visit Anaheim, including Lindsay Swanson, Wesley Kirkpatrick, and Steve Rathje, who recommended me for this project and continue to give me a platform to highlight the city.

Cherie Whyte and the Knott's Berry Farm marketing team continue to provide the berry best partnership, making it an honor to share my love of the Farm. Likewise, the collaboration between the "Berry Bloggers" has been inspiring, and I'm forever grateful for the professional and personal friendships that have bloomed.

Thank you to Chris Kent for foodie fact-checking and letting me tap into his beer insight. Kudos and appreciation are necessary for Greg Nagel for his impact on the craft beer scene in Orange County.

Thank you to the Anaheim Historical Society and stewards of the city Kevin Kidney and Jody Daily.

• •

Pour Vida

FOOD
AND DRINK

SET SAIL
FOR STRONG WATER

If you're looking for the perfect escape, set sail for the tiki bar Strong Water. The ship's manifest includes classic tiki drinks, plus originals like the molasses-y Zombie King made with rums (yup, multiple rums to make pirates proud!), lime and pineapple juices, cinnamon, and walnut and angostura bitters. Weigh anchor for a few hours and order from the rotating, seasonal dinner menu with Asian-fusion choices, like the award-winning Loco Moco Burger.

While Strong Water's food and drink make their own waves, the immersive decor adds to the experience. The interior is decorated to resemble wreckage from the fictional ship *Clementine*, lost to Davy Jones's "Locker" in 1884. Once you see the impeccable recreation, you'll understand why reservations are required and go quickly! Plan on putting your name on the list in advance and adhere to their reservation policies. Guests can also walk up and visit the shoreside dining, also known as their outdoor patio.

270 S Clementine Blvd., 714-829-4060
strongwateranaheim.com

TIP

If you're looking for more fun in the tiki, tiki, tiki room, head over to Trader Sam's Enchanted Tiki Bar at the Disneyland Hotel. Inspired by the Jungle Cruise attraction, the bar and restaurant includes fun surprises like faux rainstorms activated by your bar order.

IMMERSE YOURSELF IN A VIDEO GAME
AT REQUIEM CAFE

Escape into Requiem Cafe: Coffee, Tea, and Fantasy. The coffee shop features immersive, fantastical zones commonly seen in video games. Snuggle up with a book in the fairy tree with a themed latte like the Pumpkin King from the fall menu. Take your bubble waffle and sit in your rightful place on the throne that looks like it came from *Game of Thrones*. Sip your lemonade "magic potion" while watching anime or playing a board game with friends. This inclusive destination has something for everyone!

Requiem is a respite for patrons with diverse fandoms. Follow them on social media to stay informed of themed game or movie nights. There's even a store to pick up additional collectibles like plush stuffed animals and an area take photos in your cosplay.

280 S Clementine St., 714-844-2245
requiemcafe.com

UNPACK NEW FLAVORS
IN THE ANAHEIM PACKING DISTRICT

The Anaheim Packing District is near the heart of Downtown Anaheim, and the unique eateries will be at the heart of your foodie journey in town. You'll not go hungry with four historic areas each housing unique small businesses. Consider this your grub guide for the hot spot.

The Packing House: A historic Sunkist citrus packing plant has been transformed into a foodie haven. The multi-story food hall features a variety of 30 artisan vendors, each more droolworthy than the next. Curated restaurants and a vintage-meets-modern vibe make it a must visit when you're in town. Wondering what to eat? There's Indian-fusion food at ADYA, vegan pizza from Healthy Junk, plus comfort food from The Kroft, just to name a few.

Packard Bldg.: Park it for a while in the Packard Bldg., once a car dealership now home to Monkish Brewing. There's a tasting room and outdoor patio for summer sipping.

Farmers Park: Great meals have grown in Farmers Park. The outdoor space features restaurants like Poppy & Seed in a glass greenhouse or the lantern-adorned dim sum restaurant, 18 Folds. You'll also find year-round pop-up markets in the park. If you're visiting The Packing House with kids, grab your meal to-go and eat alfresco in Farmers Park.

MAKE Bldg.: The MAKE Bldg. will be your jam as well. The 1917 marmalade factory now houses the superhero-themed Unsung Brewery where you'll be buzzing about beers like Buzz Man. The outdoor space is a wonderful setting for sampling Central Coast wines at Pali Wine Co.

Plan on valet parking or using the city's free fleet of electric on-demand vehicles, FRAN. Request a ride from around CTR City, the downtown corridor of the city, using the A-Way WeGo app or by calling 714-490-0486.

440 S Anaheim Blvd.
anaheimpackingdistrict.com

TAP
THE LA PALMA BEER TRAIL

Plan your beer-cation in Anaheim, one of the nation's most brewery-friendly cities. Hovering in the vicinity of La Palma Avenue is a hot spot for hopheads, which allows quick access to numerous breweries. The name "La Palma Beer Trail," a phrase originally coined by OC Beer Blog's Greg Nagel, represents a dozen or so breweries centered in the area, each offering its own perks and pints.

TIP

While it's not on the La Palma Beer Trail, Green Cheek Beer Co. in Orange, CA, is worth the detour. The hoppy beers, hard seltzers, and joyful vibes will make you "Drink While Smiling." Named after loud-mouthed local parrots, Green Cheek Beer Co. is worth squawking about.

JUST A SAMPLING TO GET YOU STARTED ON YOUR TRAIL TAPPING

The Bruery Tasting Room
The Bruery is a great place to start your trek on the trail with innovative, barrel-aged beer. There are over 40 beers on tap, but you'll love the sours.
717 Dunn Way, Placentia, 714-729-2300
thebruery.com

Bottle Logic Brewing
Brewing beer is a science, so it's fitting Bottle Logic plays off the theming for its tasting room. Experiment with their Double Actuator IPA or 714 Blonde Ale.
1072 N Armando St., 714-660-2537
bottlelogic.com

Brewery X
Make sure to include Brewery X during your visit. The family- and pet-friendly brewery is a collaboration between beer professionals that has yielded exceptional beers and seltzers. You'll also find Brewery X beers at the Honda Center and Angel Stadium.
3191 E La Palma Ave., 657-999-1500
brewery-x.com

Stereo Brewing
The jams are playing and the beer is pouring at the music-inspired Stereo Brewing. Grab an ale or seltzer with friends.
950 S Via Rodeo, Placentia, 714-993-3390
stereobrewing.com

A few more spots to consider:
Broken Timbers Brewing Company, Asylum Brewing, Phantom Ales, Dueling Ducks Brewing Co., All-American Brew Works, and Honey Pot Meadery

ELEVATE YOUR EVENING
AT THE FIFTH

Atop the Grand Legacy Hotel, you'll find The FIFTH rooftop restaurant and bar. Grab light bites and a cocktail to enjoy around the fire pits on cool evenings. A popular choice is the Attitude Adjustment, a fruity, tequila-based drink. Theme your night with Tiki Tuesdays, Whiskey Wednesdays, and Taco Thursdays. Since we're taco-ing about tacos, each month their menu features a new option like a Surf & Turf.

If you're looking for energetic nightlife, The FIFTH offers live music and entertainment. The most magical element, however, is its position directly across the street from the Disney California Adventure Park. It's a wonderful spot for enjoying the nightly Disneyland fireworks unobstructed! While the fireworks are scheduled nightly for around 9:30 p.m., you'll want to get to the hotel early to park on-site. Otherwise, park at the Anaheim GardenWalk.

1650 S Harbor Blvd., 714-772-0899
thefifthoc.com

TIP
There are numerous rooftop bars around town offering scenic views and spectacular brews. Check out Top of the V at the Viv Hotel, Parkestry at the JW Marriott, or RISE Rooftop Lounge at the Westin Anaheim Resort for upscale experiences.

FEED YOUR SOUL CHICKEN AND WAFFLES
AT ROSCOE'S

Is it breakfast? Is it dinner? Whatever it is, the flavors are so, so right. Roscoe's House of Chicken and Waffles is a California-based soul food chain whose popularity spread thanks to famous fans like Stevie Wonder and President Barack Obama. They even have a special named after the former president with chicken, waffles, potato salad, and French fries. Grab that or an order of chicken thighs and waffles topped with scoops of butter and maple syrup. Wash it down with a sweet Sunrise, with orange juice and lemonade. It's the ultimate comfort food meal any time of day.

Where the combination of chicken and waffles began is up for debate, but it's great to have Roscoe's serving it up for Anaheim from 8 a.m. to 10 p.m. (12 a.m. on Saturdays).

2110 S Harbor Blvd., 714-823-4130
roscoeschickenandwaffles.com

TIP

Looking for more soul food? Check out Georgia's Restaurant for chicken, wings, black-eyed peas, and fries at the Anaheim Packing House.

RAISE A GLASS
AT COLONY WINE MERCHANT

Whether you're a sommelier or a casual wine drinker, you're welcome at Colony Wine Merchant, the inviting wine bar in Downtown Anaheim. Comfy plush armchairs fill the space, perfect for small groups to enjoy conversation or a private party. The menu features small producers with big flavor, plus artisan cheeses and bites to create a delightful evening. Even chocolate chip cookies are elevated at the Colony Wine Merchant. Indoor and outdoor seating are available, but when owner Mike Kelson grabs his guitar and microphone, you'll want to cozy up with a featured flight for the entertainment.

In addition to serving wine by the bottle or glass, there's a lovely selection for purchase in person or online. Join the wine club for four bottles thoughtfully selected and distributed at private events every other month.

280 S Lemon St., 657-208-1860
colonywinemerchant.com

START YOUR DAY WITH A SALT & BUTTER ROLL
AT OKAYAMA KOBO CAFE & BAKERY

Start your day with a crescent-shaped roll with hints of butter and salt at the Japanese cafe and bakery, Okayama Kobo. The Salt & Butter Rolls are made fresh daily from additive- and preservative-free dough, which means your morning will be light and airy, just like your breakfast.

Okayama Kobo on Center Street Promenade is our family's go-to coffeeshop and quick breakfast spot. Kids love the chocolate custard-filled buns with emoji-like characters drawn on top. If you're hoping for something savory, try my teen's favorite, The Bacon. Pair your baked goods with a cup of coffee or tea like the purple Sea Salt Taro Latte.

There's typically a line outside on weekend mornings, but it moves quickly. Take your pastries and drinks to the outdoor patio or down the street to the nearby Lemon Street Parklet.

155 W Center St. Promenade, 714-603-7332
okayamakobousa.com

VISIT A CANTINA FAR, FAR AWAY
AT OGA'S CANTINA

Looking for a watering hole that's out of this galaxy? Head to Batuu, the Star Wars–themed land inside the Disneyland Resort, where you'll find Oga's Cantina. The hot spot for bounty hunters features a menu of fantastical concoctions like the "Jedi Mind Trick," plus beers and wines on tap.

It's largely a standing room, so you can groove to the droid beats being played by DJ R-3X. It's best to secure your reservation through the official Disneyland app 60 days in advance. If your starship dropped you in Batuu with less notice, add your party to the mobile walk-up list and monitor availability.

Visiting *Star Wars: Galaxy's Edge* is a must while visiting the resort, even if *Star Wars* isn't your thing. The immersive environment is a mind-blowing recreation, plus the Rise of the Resistance attraction technology is revolutionary.

1600 S Disneyland Dr., 714-781-4636
disneyland.disney.go.com/dining/disneyland/ogas-cantina

ORDER
SALMON CHOCOLAT
AT THE ANAHEIM WHITE HOUSE

Why is the Anaheim White House restaurant famous? First, it's housed in a historic 1909 mansion that sets the stage for opulence. Next, its chef and owner Bruno Serato is a locally known philanthropist who has fed over eight million pasta dishes to needy children through his nonprofit Caterina's Club. But its fame comes from dishes like the Salmon Chocolat, a steamed Atlantic salmon with white chocolate mashed potatoes. Order the decadent dish at least once before moving onto the other steak and seafood options.

It's ideal for a date night as you eat alfresco under the patio trees, but the menu also includes family-friendly meal options if you're teaching the next generation how to enjoy the finer things in life.

887 S Anaheim Blvd., 714-772-1381
anaheimwhitehouse.com

FLIP
OVER THE ORIGINAL PANCAKE HOUSE

Let the crowd outside be a sign you're in for one of Anaheim's favorite breakfasts. The Original Pancake House started in Portland, but has been an Anaheim institution since the 1950s. The single-family home turned hotcake hotspot serves up comfort food from 6 a.m to 2 p.m. You can join a virtual waitlist on their website or line up along the sidewalk.

Fan favorites from the griddle include the Dutch Baby, a German pancake served with lemon wedges and powdered sugar, and the Apple Pancake with fresh apples and cinnamon sugar glaze. Waffles, omelets, eggs, and crepes plus other traditional favorites fill out the menu. While the restaurant has expanded to include a wheelchair accessible patio, it's largely unchanged from what Anaheimians remember.

1418 E Lincoln Ave., 714-535-9815
ophanaheim.com

TIP

Want more options to start your day? Try the Scratch Room, Huckleberry's, or Willie's Eatery for a local-approved breakfast.

MEAT UP
AT WINDSOR BROWN'S

If you're looking for a casual place to hang with buddies, "meat" them at Windsor Brown's in downtown Anaheim. The refined sandwich menu pairs the highest level of meats and artisanal bread, like the roast beef "Roast Beastly" with horseradish mayo, sharp cheddar, herb oil, heirloom tomato, and red onion on a ciabatta, plus flavorful vegetarian options and a kid's menu.

The tap list of perfectly stored and poured beers is curated with local breweries. The SoCal brewery scene is close-knit, and the team behind Windsor Brown's welcomes you to sample the best of the best brews.

This is not a typical sub shop; it's a neighborhood hangout spot with specialty sandwiches and local beers curated by industry insiders. Meat-ing up with friends on their outdoor patio should be your new weekend lunch tradition.

211 W Center St. Promenade, 714-603-7637
windsorbrowns.com

BRIGHTEN YOUR BREWS
AT RADIANT BEER CO.

Spend your sunny days "sending out light" as their tagline suggests. Head to Radiant Beer Co. where you can get both beer slushies and beer soft serve during the warmer months. Fruity tarts or dessert-inspired flavors are featured in slushie and soft serve form. Stick around for food trucks and great vibes on the large patio. It's a family-friendly space, perfect for gobbling up smashburgers and playing a round of foosball.

Radiant's tap list is ever-changing but always offers drinkable beers ranging from crisp lagers to barrel-aged stouts. They're some of the best in town, and according to The Great American Beer Festival, the best in the nation. The Anaheim-founded brewery won 2021's Best Brewer of the Year and Best Brewery in the Small, 0-250 barrels category. Even if the forecast is glum, you'll find a radiant day awaiting you at this brewery.

1566 W Lincoln Ave., 714-661-5790
radiantbeer.com

CHOW DOWN ON THE MAC DADDY OF BURGERS
AT CRAFT BY SMOKE AND FIRE

Have you walked into a barbecue restaurant and wanted one of each? If so, you'll want the MAC Rib Sandwich at Craft by Smoke and Fire. Texas toast is piled high with double smashburgers, American cheese, prime brisket, giant short rib, comeback sauce, campfire onions, burger spread, and BBQ sauce. If that sounds like too much to eat in one meal, you're right. But when you find out how delicious it all is, you'll be grateful the burger is going to last.

Since we're going big, grab a giant Bavarian pretzel to share. Wash it down with a craft cocktail made by a "band of misfit bartenders." There's even a cocktail served in a plastic bathtub, complete with floating rubber ducky.

195 W Center St. Promenade, 714-603-7194
craftbysmokeandfire.com

GRAB A JOE LATTI
AT JOE'S ITALIAN ICE

You'll find a sweet spot to treat yourself at Joe's Italian Ice, just down the street from the Disneyland Resort. The Philadelphia-style ice has come to Anaheim, and it's quickly becoming a local favorite on sunny days (and cooler ones, too!). Don't confuse this ice with a snow-cone; its consistency is closer to a sorbet than shaved ice. At Joe's, the daily menu rotates and includes a variety of flavors available, ranging from fruity to peanut butter. Try the smooth ice in a "Joe Latti," where a core of soft serve is surrounded by your choice of Italian ice. There's even a pup cup for your furry friends.

The parking lot is small in comparison to the big flavors, so be on the lookout for street parking.

2201 S Harbor Blvd., 714-703-2100
joesice.com

WANT THE SCOOP ON MORE FROZEN TREATS? HERE ARE MORE ICE CREAM SPOTS

Han's Homemade Ice Cream
440 S Anaheim Blvd., 714-520-0445
hanshomemade.com

Salt & Straw
1550 Disneyland Dr., 714-855-4321
saltandstraw.com

Sugarbuzz
6386 E Santa Ana Canyon Rd., 714-941-9059
sugarbuzzinc.com

Popbar
440 S Anaheim Blvd., 714-215-4679
pop-bar.com

ORDER A
BRUSSEL SPROUT TACO
AT POUR VIDA TORTILLAS AND TAPS

Make your mother proud and eat your brussel sprouts. Before you turn the page, let me convince you that Chef Jimmy Martinez has turned the veggie into your new favorite meal. Pour Vida Tortilla and Taps's Brussel Sprout Taco features soy-ginger glazed sprouts with queso fresco on a handmade tortilla. The top-tier tacos are vegetarian friendly, but even carnivores are going green. Order two to make a meal or sample a variety with other options like the Anaheim Burger Taco. Wash down your Brussel Sprout Tacos with a local beer on tap or a spicy margarita.

The colorful interior and outdoor patio make Pour Vida a great choice for a night out with friends. There's also a great brunch menu with bowls and concha breakfast sandwiches, plus churro pancakes that I adore.

215 S Anaheim Blvd., 714-215-4415
pvtandt.com

TREAT YOURSELF
AT HOUSE OF CHIMNEY CAKES

The city of Anaheim has German roots, but its culinary food scene is quite diverse. Take the Hungarian House of Chimney Cakes. You'll find a chimney cake at the crossroads of a churro and a donut. The dough is wrapped around a cylinder and baked to have a crispy outside and fluffy inside. Alone they're a fantastic treat, but the Anaheim dessert shop fills them with soft serve and adds a variety of toppings by hand. I'm partial to the chocolate, graham cracker, and hand-torched marshmallow of the s'mores, but Disney fans may want to add a little magic with "The Mouse" complete with Oreo ears. Vegan options are available when you opt for the pineapple Dole Whip.

Before you dig in, snap a photo of the chimney cake to share on social media (they're that pretty). But actually sharing your chimney cake? That's totally optional.

173 W Center St. Promenade, 714-603-7859
thehouseofchimneycakes.com

TIP
Looking for more globally inspired treats? Check out Tocumbo Ice Cream for homemade ice cream and paletas from authentic Mexican recipes.

SWIRL SPAGHETTI
AT MAMA COZZA'S

Italian dishes just like Mama used to make are on the menu at Mama Cozza's. The restaurant has been in business since the 1960s and saw a resurgence after an appearance on Guy Fieri's *Diners, Drive-ins, and Dives.* For longtime residents returning for another serving of Mama's Sauce, it'll seem like time has stood still. Relive the pasta dishes of yesteryear in the comfy booths set with plaid tablecloths under dark, moody lighting. The hearty portions are just like you remember, too, so swirl spaghetti while you reminisce.

It's a great spot for a throwback date night with a full bar, TVs for game day viewings, and live music. Invite the whole family to take over the banquet room to make any day one worth celebrating.

2170 W Ball Rd., 714-635-0063
mamacozzas.com

FUN FACT
Mama Cozza's was the chosen location for the launch of the GXVE beauty line by Anaheim's own Gwen Stefani.

RESERVE YOUR SEAT
AT THE CHEF'S COUNTER AT NAPA ROSE

Feast on the bounty of the Golden State at the elegant Napa Rose restaurant within Disney's Grand Californian Hotel & Spa styled to mirror the Craftsman movement. Any table at the restaurant will grant you access to upscale, wine country cuisine, but the best seat in the house is at the Chef's Counter.

The open prep kitchen is your backdrop for the night. You can order off the regular or Vitner's menu, but the true experience comes from sharing your preferences with the chef and having a tasting menu curated for you. Seats are $150 per person, plus an additional $90 for wine pairing. Call the restaurant directly two months in advance to make reservations for this unique experience as they are not available through the app.

1600 S Disneyland Dr., 714-300-7170
disneyland.disney.go.com/dining/grand-californian-hotel/napa-rose

SNAG A SLICE
FROM FOCACCIA BOI

It feels like a secret club when I get a text that Focaccia Boi's pizza order is about to drop. The home baker rose to local stardom during the pandemic selling focaccia bread, but his square, deep-dish, Detroit-style pizza is the stuff of legend. Once you try the curly pepperoni cups brimming with sprinkled Parmesan on crispy bread with caramelized crust, you'll understand why he's got an ever-growing following of loyal fans.

The pizza spots each week go quickly (hence the need for text notifications). But you can also find Focaccia Boi bread around town during select times at Colony Wine Merchant, Windsor Brown's, and Thank You Coffee.

instagram.com/focacciaboi

TIP
Missed the pizza slots for the week? You might snag Focaccia Boi's baked bread on the menu at the Colony Wine Merchant or Windsor Brown's.

WANT THE DISH ON MORE PIZZA OPTIONS? TRY ONE OF THESE!

Cortina's
2175 W Orange Ave., 714-535-1948
cortinasitalianfood.com

Italian Pizza Rosa
2825 E Lincoln Ave., 714-630-0750
italianpizzarosa.com

Marri's Pizza
1194 W Katella Ave., 714-533-1631
marrispizza.com

Pizza X
3191 E La Palma Ave., 657-999-1500
brewery-x.com

GIVE 'EM SOMETHING
TO TACO 'BOUT

Trying to pick out the best taco shop in town is like trying to pick a favorite child. So rather than get myself disowned, I'm going to share a small sampling of favorites. Whether you're looking for a sit-down restaurant or a late-night pitstop, check out a few of these restaurants and taquerias.

There are options for every price point and every craving. I adore the soy chorizo tacos from Cervantes Mexican Kitchen after the Thursday Farmers Market downtown when they are offered two for $5 or three for $7. For date night, try Urbana in the Anaheim Packing House where the vibes set you up for a great meal. But you won't want to skip smaller taquerias with cult followings, like the Little Caboose Taco Shop.

TIP

Looking for ingredients to make tacos at home? Northgate Markets is the largest chain of Mexican supermarkets in the US and traces its roots to its original Anaheim location.

Urbana Anaheim
440 S Anaheim Blvd., 714-502-0255
urbanaanaheim.com

Puesto
1040 W Katella Ave., 714-294-0362
eatpuesto.com

La Casa Garcia
531 W Chapman Ave., 714-740-1108
lacasagarcia.com

Cervantes Mexican Kitchen
201 Center St. Promenade, 714-776-8398
cervanteskitchen.com

Lindo Michoacan 2
327 S Anaheim Blvd., 714-535-0265

Tacos El Patron
516 N State College Blvd., 714-603-7446

Birrieria Guadalajara
1750 W Lincoln Ave., 714-833-5707

El Patio Drive In
2662 W Lincoln Ave., 714-826-0691

Little Caboose Taco Shop
2225 W Ball Rd., 714-780-0162

Tacos Los Cholos
821 S State College Blvd., 833-822-6777

BREW THE BLUES
AT SUNBLISS CAFE

If you could put California sunshine and blue skies in a cup, it would look a lot like the Vanilla Latte with homemade vanilla syrup at Sunbliss Cafe. The blue hue makes it totally Instagrammable—especially against the floral wall. The whole shop is adorable and the staff is incredibly friendly, but the menu is why you'll be a repeat customer.

Start your day with their specialty coffee, tea, smoothies, acai bowls, and toast. Speaking of toast, make sure to get an order of avocado toast with balsamic. Add the garlic and thank me later. Cold-pressed juices with no preservatives or fillers are available to add even more nutrients to your day. Bonus: They've got vegan, keto, and gluten-free options, too.

701 S Weir Canyon Rd., Ste. 115, 714-363-3693
sunblisscafe.com

TIP

Personalize your acai bowl in downtown Anaheim at Lazy Bird. They offer a variety of bases like traditional acai, coconut, pineapple, or mango, plus fresh fruit and other delightfully fresh toppings like nuts, butters, seeds, and more.

DRINK LEBANESE WINE
AT ROSINE'S

The American Dream isn't on the menu, but it is certainly present at Rosine's. Bringing flavors from Syria and Lebanon with her, Chef Rosine Najarian immigrated to the United States in the 1970s. Twenty years later, together with her son Hagop, she opened a small Middle Eastern restaurant in a strip mall in Anaheim Hills, where it has grown in size and popularity.

Start with mezzeh to sample a variety of spreads. Then you'll want to order the Braised Lamb Shank or Rotisserie Chicken with the famous creamy garlic sauce. As delightful as the dinner menu, the wines and spirits are also a shining star with a collection of Chateau Musar Lebanese wines in a variety of price points. There's also a bar making handcrafted cocktails. A fabulous meal with great wine is made even more memorable when Rosine's adds live music.

721 S Weir Canyon Rd., 714-283-5141
rosines.com

SPEAK EASY
AT THE BLIND RABBIT

Shush! I'm letting you in on a little secret. When you're downstairs at the Anaheim Packing House, look for sake barrels. They're actually disguising the entrance to Anaheim's own speakeasy, The Blind Rabbit. The intimate, 30-seat, Prohibition-era inspired bar serves lavish, seasonal drink and food menus plus classic cocktails (including the once again legal absinthe) that you need to experience at least once. The attentive staff can make recommendations, but Duck Confit Mac & Cheese is a solid choice. The dimly lit and immersive atmosphere shines a light on expertly crafted beverages.

It's ideal for a date night or small party. Plan for a 90-minute visit, and make sure to secure your reservations online two weeks in advance. Dress sharply and talk softly when you visit.

440 S Anaheim Blvd., Ste. 104
theblindrabbit.com

TASTE THE TWIST
OF DON CHURRO GOMEZ

The Anaheim Marketplace boasts the title of being Orange County's largest indoor swap meet. You'll find clothing, sports equipment, shoes, accessories, the list goes on and on. But you'll also find Don Churro Gomez. You don't know how lucky you are!

Churros are just better in Anaheim (sorry, Walt Disney World) especially when they incorporate decades-old family recipes like they do at Don Churro Gomez. The loop of fried dough can be topped with ice cream (vanilla, strawberry, or butter pecan) to add even more sweetness to the crispy traditional. Add a drizzle of cajeta on top.

The food truck often has a line as their churros are made fresh and are highly coveted. It's largely standing room (if a parking lot counts as a room), but the soft, fluffy churros are worth it.

1440 S Anaheim Blvd., 714-717-7946
donchurrosgomez.com

GIMME SUGAR
AT RALPH BRENNAN'S JAZZ KITCHEN

They're messy, but so worth it. Grab an order of beignets from Ralph Brennan's Jazz Kitchen. The French-style donuts are covered in powdered sugar (hence the mess) and served hot in orders of 4, 6, or 10. You can grab them to-go from the JK Express, now called Beignets Expressed, to enjoy alfresco at the outdoor seating or continue exploring the Downtown Disney District.

Beignets are also available within the Disneyland Resort. If you haven't heard: Calories don't count in food that is Mickey-shaped. Find them at the Mint Julep Bar in the French Quarter.

After your sugar rush at Ralph Brennan's Jazz Kitchen Beignets Expressed, enjoy live music throughout the shopping center. You'll find Disney stores like World of Disney and the Disney Home store, plus other souvenirs, clothing, and footwear.

1590 Disneyland Dr., 714-776-5200
beignetsexpressed.com

HOLE UP WITH A DOZEN DONUTS FROM THESE SHOPS AROUND THE AREA

Zombee Donuts
802 E Chapman Ave., Fullerton, 714-879-1078
zombeedonut.com

Sidecar Doughnuts & Coffee
270 E 17th St., Ste. 18, Costa Mesa, 949-873-5424
sidecardoughnuts.com

Randy's Donuts
2232 E 17th St., Santa Ana, 657-900-2885
randysdonuts.com

SHAKE IT UP
AT BLACK TAP CRAFT BURGERS & BEERS

Street vibes with a sweet side await you at at Black Tap Craft Burgers & Beers, the quick casual restaurant in Downtown Disney. Dig into their burgers like the Greg Norman with half pound of Wagyu beef and topped with a house-made buttermilk dill dressing, blue cheese, and arugula. Then add fries, fried pickles, or mozzarella triangles.

But save room because the CrazyShakes are literally over the top. Premium milkshakes are the base of the concoction. Then they're topped with an array of sweets from cotton candy to entire slices of cake like The Cakeshake, a cake batter–flavored shake with a slice of funfetti atop its sprinkled rim. If you're grabbing a shake to-go, take advantage of the walk-up window.

Expect resort-level pricing and a plan to share milkshakes.

1540 S Disneyland Dr., 657-276-2498
blacktap.com/location/anaheim

SWEETEN YOUR DAY WITH MORE MILKSHAKES
Ruby's Diner
Shooby Dooby to the Five Points location for classic shakes.
1128 W Lincoln Ave., 714-635-7829
rubys.com/location/anaheim

Sugarbuzz
Home to the Unicorn Hot Chocolate
6386 E Santa Ana Canyon Rd., 714-941-9059
sugarbuzzinc.com

SAY "OMG!"
AT OMG DESSERT LOUNGE

Don't let its unassuming location in a gas station parking lot deter you. OMG Dessert Lounge sells the macarons I bribe my children with, the ones they pick out for their birthdays, the ones I secretly sneak out and buy when they are at school and eat by myself (sorry, kids). The passion fruit is a family favorite, but I'd grab a six-pack to try a few more flavors to find your favorite with flavors like Earl Grey, Coconut, and Taro, plus fruity options.

Macarons don't have a long shelf-life, so you'll want to go back to OMG Dessert Lounge daily from 12–8 p.m. to keep a supply on hand. OMG Dessert Lounge also sells ice cream, boba, and cannoli. I won't judge you if you opt for the best of both worlds and top your ice cream scoop with a macaron. Say it's research and snap a selfie in front of their Instagram wall. Seating is limited, but you can take your treats across the street to Farmers Park.

301 S Anaheim Blvd., 714-603-7525
omgdessertlounge.com

TIP

Macarons are having a moment. Across the street Le Petit Paris has a case filled with delightful treats, including macarons. Honey & Butter in Irvine, sells super cute character macarons. One of my favorite Disneyland Resort treats is the Raspberry Rose Mickey Macaron at the Jolly Holiday Bakery Cafe.

Boysenberry Festival

MUSIC
AND ENTERTAINMENT

MAXIMIZE THE MAGIC
AT THE DISNEYLAND RESORT

It wouldn't be a guide to Anaheim without sprinkling bits in about the Disneyland Resort. While I could easily talk your Mickey ears off about the theme park, instead I'm going to offer a few ways to maximize the magic while visiting.

Download the App: Ahead of your visit, download the official Disneyland app. It'll be your guide throughout your day with maps, wait times, access to photos, and allow you to mobile order meals and snacks.

Rope Drop: Get an early start by planning to be through the park gates 30 minutes before Disneyland officially opens. You'll be positioned to jump-start your day and can snag shorter wait times for E-ticket rides by getting there first.

Mobile Order and Checkout: As I mentioned, you can use the app to order your food in advance. Select a window when you'd like to eat and let them know when you've arrived. You can even mobile order snacks like Dole Whip to save more time.

Similarly, you can do a mobile checkout when souvenir shopping.

Rider Swap: If visiting with a child not tall enough for a ride, tell the cast member at the entrance you'd like to do a Rider Swap. Adults can then ride one at a time without having to get back in line.

Pick Must Do's: Ahead of your visit, identify the must do attractions or activities for your party. Then be flexible! You'll uncover fun if you're not stuck to a rigid schedule. Genie+ can assist with itineraries for your visit.

I would strongly recommend adding Rise of the Resistance, Mickey & Minnie's Runaway Railway, Incredicoaster, and WEB SLINGERS: A Spider-Man Adventure to your adventure.

Incorporate Down Time: I would recommend spending three days at the Disneyland Resort, if possible. This will eliminate the feelings of needing to get it all done in one day. Regardless of your travel plans, incorporate some down time in your plans. The Enchanted Tiki Room, for example, allows you to rest your feet in AC for a spell.

HONOR THE BERRY THAT STARTED IT ALL
AT KNOTT'S BERRY FARM

A humble berry stand turned into America's first theme park in the neighboring city of Buena Park. Anaheim horticulturist Rudolph Boysen is credited with the creation of the boysenberry, a blend between a raspberry, blackberry, and loganberry. During the Great Depression, Walter Knott cultivated the plant with great success. Another economic success befell the Knott family when Mrs. Cordelia Knott's fried chicken dinners served on her wedding china for a whopping 65 cents went viral. The lines for her dinners required entertainment for those waiting in line, and the Knott's Berry Farm theme park was born!

Each spring, Knott's celebrates the berry that started it all with its annual Boysenberry Festival serving dozens of boysenberry-inspired dishes. Grab a Tasting Card to sample boysenberry dishes like Boysenberry Sausage or Elote. Ditch the kids and take advantage of the beer and wine samplings in the Wilderness Dance Hall.

Additional entertainment and berry-themed fun is served by the bushel. Craft vendors, live shows, games, and boysenberry food items make it a must visit each spring.

8039 Beach Blvd., Buena Park, 714-220-5200
knotts.com

CHECK OUT THE NUMEROUS THEME PARKS IN AND AROUND ANAHEIM

Disneyland Resort
1313 Disneyland Dr.
disneyland.disney.go.com

Knott's Berry Farm
8039 Beach Blvd., Buena Park, 714-220-5200
knotts.com

Adventure City
Perfect for younger children
1238 S Beach Blvd., 714-236-9300
adventurecity.com

LEGOLAND
1 Legoland Dr., Carlsbad, 888-690-5346
legoland.com/california/homepage

Universal Studios
Ideal for pop culture and movie fans
100 Universal City Plaza, Universal City, 800-864-8377
universalstudioshollywood.com

Six Flags Magic Mountain
26101 Magic Mountain Pkwy., Valencia, 661-255-4100
sixflags.com/magicmountain

SeaWorld
500 Sea World Dr., San Diego, 619-222-4SEA
seaworld.com/san-diego

Sesame Place
Perfect for preschoolers
2052 Entertainment Cir., Chula Vista, 619-943-ELMO
sesameplace.com/san-diego

FLOAT ON DOWN
FOR THE ANAHEIM HALLOWEEN PARADE

In 1924, with Babe Ruth as its marshal, the first Anaheim Halloween Parade rolled down through town. The centennial tradition brings throngs of people to Broadway to watch vintage-inspired floats that pay homage to designs of yesteryear. Andy Anaheim, the city's mascot, joins characters like the Rocket Witch and a jack-o-lantern man in checkered pants for the beloved parade. Make sure to save the Saturday before Halloween for the parade and fall festival.

Ahead of the parade, head to Downtown Anaheim for a fall festival. Community booths, costume contests (even one for pups!), music, and crafts start the Halloween celebration. But you'll want to get your seats early on the parade route to watch the floats, plus community groups, classic cars, and more.

Broadway and Anaheim Blvd.
anaheimfallfestival.org

EAT A DEEP-FRIED OREO
AT THE OC FAIR

Deep fried everything! Fair food is a must each summer when the Orange County Fair returns for a month of entertainment. Grab some fried Oreos, funnel cake, or oversized corn dogs before exploring the blue ribbon community contests and the adorable piglets. The pig races are a must see! Go down the gigantic slide or up to check out the views of Costa Mesa, California, from atop the Ferris Wheel. Make sure to stock up on deep-fried Oreos to share with the stars as you secure tickets for the summer concert series at the Pacific Amphitheatre or Hangar.

Hoping for a bigger budget for your fair feasting? Make sure to follow the OC Fair on social media for information on discounts like free admission with donation for local charities. Kids can also earn free rides by completing summer reading.

88 Fair Dr., Costa Mesa, 714-708-1500
ocfair.com

ROCK OUT
AT THE HOUSE OF BLUES ANAHEIM

First we eat, and then we rock. The House of Blues Anaheim is located at the Anaheim GardenWalk, an outdoor dining and entertainment center located down the street from the Disneyland Resort.

Ahead of your show, order some Voodoo Shrimp and a Southern-inspired entree like Jambalaya from the restaurant and bar. Then it's time for the show to start. The concert venue is made up of several rooms with differing capacities, plus tons of art on display throughout to lift your soul. There's even a catwalk to offer a bird eye's view of your favorite bands on stage. Whether you're up in the VIP Foundation Room or up close and personal on the floor, you're in for a rockin' night.

There's parking available in the Anaheim GardenWalk structure with validation available.

400 W Disney Way, Ste. 337, 714-778-2583
houseofblues.com/anaheim

TIP
Looking for more places to rock? Chain Reaction is a smaller, all-ages club on Lincoln Avenue that has a calendar filled with punk, indie, and other shows.

GET AN AUTOGRAPH
AT WONDERCON

If you're a fan of comics or pop culture, you'll want to grab a badge to WonderCon. The three-day convention is operated by the same company that hosts ComicCon in San Diego. Held at the Anaheim Convention Center, WonderCon is your ticket to getting autographs from award-winning writers, illustrators, and other creators. Line up for the autographs you want in advance to increase your odds as space is limited (check their official website of who to anticipate).

One draw for attendees is the cosplay component. Many will congregate outside the ACC for group photos. Excelsior!

If you're looking to expand your autograph collection, check out other conventions coming to the ACC. NAMM (National Association of Music Merchants), VidCon, Natural Products Expo West, and D23 are just a few on the convention center's calendar.

800 W Katella Ave., 714-765-8950
comic-con.org/wca

TWO-STEP
AT THE RANCH SALOON

Saddle up for a great night. Included in the MICHELIN Guide California, The RANCH Restaurant is a rustic steakhouse and bar, serving up premium large format steak like the 58-ounce Cowboy Ribeye. The seasonally driven menu is complemented by an extensive and expertly curated wine list. But the fun doesn't stop when dessert is done.

The restaurant and bar is adjacent to their saloon, an upscale country music and dancing venue. If your cowboy boots are a little rusty, visit Thursday through Saturday nights when instructors offer free dance lessons. On Friday and Saturday nights, you'll enjoy local live bands playing country music for you to practice line dancing. If you are not dining at the restaurant, there is a bar menu with items to fuel your fancy footwork like burgers and wings.

1025 E Ball Rd., Ste. 101B, 714-817-4200
theranch.com

CATCH
A BROADWAY SHOW
AT THE SEGERSTROM

Broadway is closer than you think! The hottest shows go to the Segerstrom Center for the Arts in Costa Mesa. The modern center presents a spectacular line-up of top-notch entertainment year-round, but my personal favorite events are the Broadway shows. If you're interested in enjoying multiple shows throughout the year, consider bundling tickets through one of their subscriptions. There are numerous restaurants nearby at South Coast Plaza, plus concessions for purchase inside the theater.

Parking in attached garages is easy and runs at $15. It's recommended to arrive an hour before showtime. Their musicals typically have a photo opportunity in the lobby, plus you'll have time to use the restroom (lines during intermission can get long). Enjoy a night of spectacular theater and culture at the Segerstrom.

600 Town Center Dr., Costa Mesa, 714-556-2787
scfta.org

PICK YOUR DINNER
AT TANAKA FARMS

Strawberries, watermelons, pumpkins, oh my! All year-round, family-owned Tanaka Farms offers reservations for the public to access their grounds for wagon rides and fresh tastes of their produce, which are also available at their produce stand. The raw sweet corn is phenomenal! The U-Pick Activities are popular family outings, but not the only offering.

You'll find pumpkin patches and Christmas trees for the holidays. Make sure to add a Farm-to-Table Cookout to your spring agenda. You'll be directed to a tour through the farm, picking fresh produce as you go, and then enjoy a grilled meal alfresco using the same fruits and veggies you've just been picking. Both daytime and evening events are scheduled, with prices ranging from $34–$59 for each adult.

5380 ¾ University Dr., Irvine, 949-653-2100
tanakafarms.com

TIP
Want to enjoy the produce regularly? Consider signing up for the CSA, or Community Supported Agriculture, program for a subscription to farm fresh fruits and veggies.

SWASHBUCKLE YOUR WAY
TO PIRATE'S DINNER ADVENTURE

Yo ho! It's a pirate's dinner adventure for me. Bring your scalliwags to the high-action dinner theater in Buena Park for a night of swashbuckling, acrobatics, and maybe even romance on the high seas. The shows (regular, Halloween's *Vampirates*, and Christmas's *Pirates Take Christmas*) are set on a Spanish galleon, surrounded by water. Guests are invited up throughout the show to help their pirate with various tasks for an engaging night of dinner theater. It's a great birthday outing for young pirates.

A three-course dinner is included with admission, starting at $65.95 for adults and $38.95 for children. The vegetarian ravioli is lovely, and I get it every time I visit. Additionally, there's a bar with themed cocktails.

7600 Beach Blvd., Buena Park, 714-690-1497
piratesdinneradventureca.com

TIP
Looking for additional dinner theater options? Cheer on your knight at Medieval Times Dinner & Tournament or be amazed at Kip Barry's Cabaret, a magic and variety show, at the Anaheim GardenWalk.

SOAR ABOVE THE OC
ON THE GREAT PARK BALLOON

If you want to see Orange County, take to the skies! The Great Park in Irvine hosts free rides in a gigantic orange balloon that will take you 400 feet up for a 360-degree look at the area from the comfort of a gondola. While technically not a hot air balloon (the 118-foot-tall orange balloon is filled with helium), you'll be soaring above the park and gazing down on most of the OC and even see glimmers of Los Angeles on a good day of visibility. The ride is offered on a first-come, first-served basis with weather permitting.

The Great Park is also home to a vintage-inspired carousel charging $3 a ride. Make it a full day of outdoor adventures with the balloon and carousel rides, plus exploring the play complexes, Farmers Market, and trails. Shade chairs and umbrellas are available to rent.

8000 Great Park Blvd., Irvine, 949-724-6247
cityofIrvine.org/great-park/great-park-balloon-carousel

TAKE YOUR SEAT
AT CHANCE THEATER

Take a seat at a local theater with a purpose. Chance Theater is Anaheim's official resident theater where you'll catch a variety of entertainment ranging from socially conscious plays to family-friendly shows. Expect titles you know like *Rent* to workshops of brand new plays by their resident playwright. It offers an affordable entry point for the live arts so more community members can access the creativity and talent of local artists through moving productions in an intimate setting.

If you're looking for a night out with friends, hit up the Happy Hour for a $3 beer or glass of wine before a night of stand-up comedy on Tuesdays. For younger theater lovers, check out the children's book series *Fancy Nancy* come to life on stage at Chance.

5522 E La Palma Ave., 888-455-4212
chancetheater.com

TIP
From Anaheim, you'll have easy access to a variety of spectacular theaters. Consider the landmark of the Hollywood Pantages Theatre or Segerstrom Center for the Arts to catch popular Broadway shows.

CAPTURE THE MAGIC
OF DISNEY ON ICE

Pair incredible show-stopping moments with the emotional storytelling Disney does best. When Mickey and his pals skate into the Honda Center for Disney on Ice, we know it's a must-do family outing. The productions are bigger and, dare I say it, even more magical than what I remember from my own childhood. In addition to seeing beloved characters in top-notch musical ice performances, Disney on Ice now features aerial stunts, cutting-edge entertainment technology, and pyrotechnics. Recent shows have also incorporated increasing audience participation, even getting volunteers onto the ice for an unforgettable memory.

The shows' plots and character appearances vary during each tour. Dress in your Mickey ears and warm clothes and be ready to be awestruck and emotional all at the same time. Arrive early to grab souvenirs and snacks.

2695 E Katella Ave., 800-844-3545
disneyonice.com

SEE THE STARS
AT CITY NATIONAL GROVE OF ANAHEIM

If you're picking up on old Hollywood vibes, you're in the right spot. The City National Grove of Anaheim brings a variety of entertainment and tinsel outside of Tinseltown. Musical icons including Prince and Stevie Nicks have performed there, and today's line-up continues to be stellar. Catch hot artists, tribute bands, and a line-up of family entertainment in the 1,700-seat venue. Add the Anaheim Ballet's annual presentation of *The Nutcracker* to your holiday bucket list. If you're looking to gift live music, they also offer package deals for shows throughout the year.

Parking is a breeze, but plan on arriving early if there are events at Angel Stadium or the Honda Center. There's an extensive outdoor welcoming area, plus lobby for purchasing drinks and other concessions. Inside you'll enjoy your favorite artists in a smaller venue.

2200 E Katella Ave., 714-712-2700
citynationalgroveofanaheim.com

POP OVER
TO BUBBLEFEST AT DISCOVERY CUBE

Curious scientists in training will love the Discovery Cube. The two-story hands-on museum explores everything from recycling to earthquakes daily from 10 a.m.–5 p.m. Don't miss the annual springtime Bubblefest when you can get down and dirty with good, clean fun! Kids can ride paddle boats, explore the patio area filled with bubble activities, a Bubble Wall, and more.

The sudsy science comes to a peak during the 45-minute Mega Bubblefest Laser Show where a renowned bubble artist (yes, that's a thing) takes the stage for a high-energy bubble art performance with music, lasers, and un-bubble-able tricks. Tickets start at $26.95 for children and $31.95 for adults, plus $6 for parking. Premier tickets include exclusive seating and early fast pass entry for the show.

2500 N Main St., 714-542-2823
discoverycube.org

TIP
Members get early access to tickets, plus entry to exclusive events. It's a great option for homeschooling families or those looking to explore the big world with little ones.

CRAFT A GREAT NIGHT
AT CRAFT & ARTS

This isn't your average paint night. Other paint nights may involve a glass of wine and your best attempt to replicate your instructor's artwork. That's a great set-up, but this contains a little more messy glory and a whole lot more opportunity.

Craft & Arts "Not Your Average Paint Night" encourages you to unleash the inner artist (even if you don't consider yourself an artist) through creation of a one-of-a-kind collage. Held at breweries around Anaheim and Orange County, the hands-on art experience starts with a beer. You'll learn about both craft beer and the craft you're about to create from a charismatic maker. And then you're off, inspired by the possibilities of paint, wood, and mixed material. You do not need to be an artist to create art. Just come and be willing to try something new.

Make it a date night or bring your pals for a paint-ish party that is as unique as you are. Tickets are $40 and include your first pour from the brewery.

Anaheim and surrounding Orange County cities
craft-and-arts.com

ENTER THE FOG
AT KNOTT'S SCARY FARM

The fog rolls into Knott's Berry Farm every Halloween. For 50 years, the haunting has been a popular spooky season destination. One thousand monsters have taken over Scare Zones and themed mazes. There's nowhere to hide from sliding ghouls and clowns. Inside the mazes, you'll find even more startling shrieks and screams with the incorporation of masterful storytelling and modern technology like animatronic monsters, plus light and digital projections.

Fill the night of terror with sinister shows and pop-up experiences. Plus, the theme park fills its menus with terrifying treats and spooky, savory meals.

The separate-ticket event is designed for guests 13+. Weekend evenings do sell out, especially as Halloween nears. To maximize your time, consider adding the Fright Lane Pass to skip the maze lines. Another option is to enjoy the Boo-fet, the Halloween buffet that grants early access to select mazes plus photo opportunities with monsters ahead of the rope drop.

8039 Beach Blvd., Buena Park, 714-220-5200
knotts.com/events/scary-farm

TIP

Are those monsters lurking during the rinse cycle? Streaks on your windshield? EEK! The Haunted Car Wash is a unique spine-chilling offering. Pay per car and lock your doors. Otherwise you may find yourself driving some haunting hitchhikers. Buy your tickets online at tunnelofterroroc.com for the screams and suds once locations are announced.

They do sell out!

GET ON THE NICE LIST
AT THE GRAND CALIFORNIAN HOTEL & SPA

The Craftsman-style Grand Californian Hotel & Spa at the Disneyland Resort offers grandeur with a sprinkling of pixie dust, but you don't need to be a hotel guest to experience the magic. One of my favorite times to visit is during the holiday season when Santa Claus visits the hotel lobby for free visits and photos. After getting yourself on the Nice List with Santa, spend some time enjoying the hotel's entertainment and sweet treats.

A gigantic replica of the hotel made entirely out of gingerbread is on display during the holidays in the hotel's lobby. Can you spot all of the hidden Mickeys throughout the display? Make it an even sweeter visit with a baked treat or spiked libation available for purchase from the holiday cart in the lobby. If you see gingerbread Mickeys available, they're pure magic.

1600 S Disneyland Dr., 714-635-2300
disneyland.disney.go.com/grand-californian-hotel

TIP

This isn't the only place to find hidden Mickeys. Throughout the Disneyland Resort, imagineers have hidden Mickeys for the delight of eagle-eyed guests.

SPRING OVER
TO THE FLOWER FIELDS

Rainbow rows of ranunculus fill the 55-acre Northern San Diego destination, The Flower Fields, each spring. Tickets are available online for entrance, and I would recommend adding the tractor wagon ride when you arrive. This will grant you an overview of the radiant flowers. There's plenty for little ones to do including a play area, maze, and themed gardens. Wear your spring styles and strike a pose (just don't trample flowers in search of the perfect shot). You will be walking through a farm.

Whether you've got a green thumb or not, you'll be inspired by the greenhouses and displays. You can shop for your garden needs at the Armstrong Garden Center on-site.

When visiting from Anaheim, consider spending the day exploring the outlets or staying in Carlsbad to enjoy the LEGOLAND Resort.

5704 Paseo del Norte, Carlsbad, 760-431-0352
theflowerfields.com

TIP

In years with good rainfall, Orange County's cities may experience a super bloom of wildflowers. These colorful occurrences make hiking around Anaheim even more rewarding.

SPORTS
AND RECREATION

PLAY LIKE KOBE
AT THE KOBE BRYANT
MEMORIAL DREAM COURT

Pick up a game and honor legendary Laker Kobe Bryant at the "Dream Court." The basketball court constructed at Pearson Park features a full-sized court as a tribute to Kobe and his daughter Gianna ("Gigi") who both tragically passed away in a helicopter accident. A large butterfly is the backdrop for a mural bearing their pictures and a reminder to "Play Gigi's Way." There's no fee for using the popular court.

Cool down after your game by strolling Pearson Park. There's a cactus garden and duck pond, plus tennis courts and grass area for baseball or soccer if you're ready to challenge your buddies to a rematch after your basketball game. During the summer, the public pool opens for community swimming and the amphitheater welcomes a variety of affordable family entertainment.

400 N Harbor Blvd., 714-765-5155
anaheim.net

GO ON STRIKE
AT SPLITSVILLE

Looking for fun that's right up your alley? Check out Splitsville Luxury Lanes, the upscale bowling alley located within the Downtown Disney District. The restaurant and bowling alley blend retro designs with a modern feel in two stories of restaurant space and 20 lanes. The Mickey and Minnie etched bowling balls give it a touch of Disney magic.

Splitsville is a great family outing, but you can just as easily make it a date night with their elevated menu and bar. Get pizza and burgers, or opt for sushi and a Watermelon Smash with watermelon-infused moonshine to enjoy alfresco on their patio where live music regularly fills the air.

Parking for the Downtown Disney District is $10 for the first hour, and validation applies afterward. The outdoor shopping and dining area does not require theme park admission.

1530 S Disneyland Dr., 657-276-2440
splitsvillelanes.com

TIP

Looking for authentically vintage bowling? Head to Linbrook Bowl on the corner of Lincoln and Brookhurst. The look remains largely unchanged since its opening in 1958, and the neon signage is out of this league cool.

CHILL OUT
AT ANAHEIM ICE

The Rinks—Anaheim Ice is a great place to chill. The ice skating facility, which previously served as the training and practice center for the Anaheim Ducks, features both Olympic and NHL regulation sized rinks. Check their website for public skate sessions and lessons to channel your inner Wayne Gretzky or Michelle Kwan. Public skating is $15, plus $6 for skate rental. New to the ice? Rent a seal-shaped skate aid for an additional fee (or hang onto the side for dear life like I do).

Add to the fun of the skate rink by playing games at the small arcade or picking up snacks like fresh popcorn from the snack bar. You can also pick up clothes, gear, bags, and more at the on-site pro shop.

Some street parking is available, but there is also a parking structure down the street with eligible validation from the skating rink.

300 W Lincoln Ave., 714-535-7465
anaheimice.therinks.com

TIP
If all that skating worked up a big appetite, keep it cool and walk down the street to PokiNometry to build your own poki bowl.

MAKE IT A HOMERUN VISIT
AT ANGEL STADIUM

Root, root, root for the Angels at Angel Stadium. Start your tailgating at Golden Road Brewery for great burgers, beers like the Melon Cart, and outdoor yard games. Then head across the street to watch the Halos. Parking is available at the stadium for $20 and also from surrounding businesses. I recommend getting there early to snap a photo with the giant baseball hat and to score any souvenirs (check the schedule to see if any free souvenirs are being given to fans as supplies are limited). I highly recommend any ballpark snack served in a souvenir helmet like the nachos layered with all the toppings or an ice cream sundae. If you're looking for something more than typical stadium fare, X marks the spot with Brewery X's sit down restaurant offering fantastic grub and craft beers on the Club Level. On select Saturday nights, you'll enjoy a fireworks display for free after the game.

Want to hit your fandom out of the park? Get your baseball fix by taking a 75-minute tour of the stadium for $12 select days April through September when Angels are away. Game day tours are also available.

2000 E Gene Autry Way, 714-940-2000
mlb.com/angels

GRIND AND SLIDE
AT ANAHEIM WEST SKATEPARK

Started in Anaheim by brothers Paul and Jim Van Doren in 1966, Vans quickly became the preferred footwear for skateboarders thanks to the sticky soles and rugged construction. The iconic checkerboard still holds a place in local hearts and closets. The infusion of skate culture is embedded in Anaheim, so you'll want to put your best foot forward at local skate parks like Anaheim West Skatepark at Brookhurst Park.

The park's moonscape earned the nickname "Sadlands" by early skaters who would ride through the playground. Today the park has a kidney-shaped pool, plus craters to pay homage to the Sadlands.

The nostalgic and unique nature of Brookhurst Park earns it a top spot, but Ponderosa Park is a popular destination for skaters.

2271 W Crescent St., 714-765-5155
anaheim.net/facilities/facility/details/brookhurst-park-99

TIP
Looking for additional iconic parks? Take flight at Boysen Park a.k.a. "Airplane Park" or head to Garden Grove, CA, to visit the water wonderland of Atlantis Park.

TAKE A HIKE
AT OAK CANYON NATURE CENTER

If you ever need a quick trip into nature to recharge, the Oak Canyon Nature Center is perfect. The 58-acre park features easy trails, including a stroller and wheelchair-friendly "Heritage Trail." Explore the oak woodland, walk alongside the year-round running stream, and even see a mine exhibit. The Oak Canyon Nature Center is a family favorite with a themed play area where young children can pretend to be animals they'll see at Oak Canyon. If your little nature lovers are looking for more fun, check out the summer day camp.

Make sure to visit the John J. Collier Interpretive Center, a small museum with live animals and exhibits. Admission is free, but donations are accepted. Restrooms, picnic tables, and parking are available.

6700 E Walnut Canyon Rd., 714-998-8380
anaheim.net/1096/oak-canyon-nature-center

TIP
Visit a grove of redwood trees after an easy hike through Carbon Canyon Regional Park in Brea, CA.

FLY
TO THE HONDA CENTER

Fly to the Honda Center to cheer on Anaheim's mighty NHL team, the Ducks. The puck dropped for the first time in 1993, and the Ducks (previously named the Mighty Ducks after the Disney movie) have been a highlight for sports fans ever since. If you're looking for a pre-game, consider JT Schmid's across the street for a selection of microbrews and American fare. The Ducks' mascot Wild Wing is ready to get the party started, so snap a photo with his statue out front. It's not hard to keep it going with Brewery X's specially branded beers, Duck Beer and Quack IPA, available for Biergarten members (single-day passes are also available). The Honda Center is also home to a full calendar of events from top musicians to family entertainment.

2695 E Katella Ave., 714-704-2400
hondacenter.com

TIP
The center is part of a massive expansion, ocV!BE, scheduled to open in 2024 with housing, dining, shopping, and public spaces.

WIPEOUT
AT THE ADVENTURE LAGOON

Never has wiping out been more fun. The aqua agility park at the Adventure Lagoon puts you on a floating obstacle course where you can climb a 10-foot wall, race down a 16.5-foot slide, and bounce on an inflatable dome. The freshwater lagoon also features other water activities like pedal boats and kayaks, making it appropriate for swimmers of all ages. Open during the spring and summer, you'll want to bring your SPF to soak up Anaheim's sunshine. But there are lounge chairs and shade.

Pricing starts at $30 for the full day, but you'll want to add the obstacle course for an hour for an additional $10. You can purchase your tickets and fill out the required waiver in advance to secure your spot. Minors must be accompanied by an adult to visit.

3255 E Miraloma Ave., 714-983-7314
theadventurelagoon.com

HIT A HOLE IN ONE
AT THE ANAHEIM HILLS GOLF COURSE

For the record, the only golf I can manage includes windmills and water fountain obstacles. But for those who are hitting the links outside of the local mini golf Camelot (or Scam-a-lot as we called it as kids), head to one of the local courses like the Anaheim Hills Golf Course. The par-71 course features a rolling, tree-lined course. It's a challenging course but with beautiful views of the surrounding hillside.

If you're looking for a budget-friendly option, check out the walkable Dad Miller Golf Course, which was the home course for Tiger Woods as a high schooler. Another choice is The Islands Golf Center with 13 floating island targets. Clubs are available to rent at the driving range, making it a great first stop as you're working your way up to the green jacket.

6501 Nohl Ranch Rd., 714-998-3041
anaheimhillsgc.com

FLOAT DOWN THE LAZY RIVER
AT SOAK CITY

Splash into summer at Knott's Soak City in neighboring Buena Park. The seasonal water park has a lot to offer sun worshippers and thrill seekers. One highlight is Sunset River, the 1,780-foot-long lazy river that bends throughout the heart of the park. Grab an inner tube and float the day away for the ultimate relaxation. While you leisurely make your way down the lazy river, there are tons of other water attractions for the kids like free-fall water slides, wave pool, and water zone for preschoolers.

Want to make it a true summer oasis? Rent a personal cabana for your group for the day. In addition to shade coverage, you'll have meal service and personal use of inner tubes for the lazy river and other attractions. Hot tip: The ground gets hot! Bring sandals or water shoes, plus towels and sunscreen.

8039 Beach Blvd., Buena Park, 714-220-5200
knotts.com/soak-city

TAKE OVER THE TRACK
AT K1 SPEED

These aren't gussied up lawn mowers. K1 Speed offers high-performance go-karts on an indoor track. Put yourself in the driver's seat for a race around the professionally designed asphalt track using skill and live ride information. Employees assist as well to ensure you're getting to the checkered flag fast!

The higher speeds and thrilling turns make it a great option for older children (48 inches tall or above), teens, and date nights. Junior karts and adult karts race separately for safety, but I recommend grabbing a group to see which of your friends can make it to the podium!

You pay per race, and packages are available. When you're not racing, keep your competitive streak alive in the arcade. Food and drinks are also available for purchase in the Paddock Lounge.

1000 N Edward Ct., 714-632-6999
k1speed.com/anaheim-location.html

CATCH A WAVE
IN HUNTINGTON BEACH

If you're looking for a Southern California destination, nothing screams SoCal more than a day in Huntington Beach, also known as Surf City USA. From Anaheim, you can head down Beach Boulevard to spend the day catching a wave in the Pacific, playing beach volleyball, biking along the paved beach path, and ending the day with s'mores over the bonfire pits. Plan your visit to catch one of the numerous events held on the beach, like the US Open of Surfing.

Looking to spend a full day in sunny HB? Add in a visit to Pacific City, the outdoor retail and dining center with views of the ocean. Visit the International Surfing Museum Thursdays through Sundays from 11 a.m.–5 p.m. for a peek at surf memorabilia and culture. Another popular destination is the pier, one of the longest on the West Coast, which offers select dining, shopping, and fishing.

Huntington Beach
surfcityusa.com

LEVEL UP
AT ARCADE MISSION CONTROL

Ready to relive your childhood? Grab your quarters and head to Arcade Mission Control where it's the '80s every day. Located on the second story of Santa Ana's McFadden Public Market is the epic pinball and vintage arcade. There are tons of variously themed machines, including throwbacks that'll bring a smile to your face. While my personal skills won't warrant any accolades, there are tournaments to join to impress your own friends.

And because we're grown up now, there's a bar with beer on tap and video game–themed-cocktails. As a bonus, the McFadden Public Market is also home to a tiki-themed speakeasy. If you're looking for a night out, check out Weekend Blast Off nights, featuring live DJs, dancing, and games.

515 N Main St., Santa Ana, 657-232-3338
mcfaddenmarket.com/arcade-mission-control

TIP
You don't need to be royalty to take the top score at the arcade at Camelot Golfland, located inside a castle. You'll also find lazer tag inside, plus minigolf, bumper boats, and go karts outdoors.

TWEET ABOUT THE BIRDS YOU SEE
AT ANAHEIM COVES

The Anaheim Coves feature a paved trail along the Santa Ana River, great for a leisurely stroll. The path is approximately 2.5 miles with views of the gated river and nearby mountains. Keep your eyes peeled while you walk the coves for a wide array of birds, including pelicans, double-crested cormorants, and geese. You'll likely see bunnies and lizards along the way as well. The nature park has educational signage along the pathway with benches along the way to enjoy the views and share photos of the wildlife you've seen.

The Anaheim Coves are a great choice for families, too. There's a dinosaur-themed play area for children with climbing structures plus sand to unearth "artifacts." The park is open from dusk to dawn with public parking and restrooms available.

2916 E Lincoln Ave., 714-765-5155
anaheim.net/facilities/facility/details/anaheim-coves-92

SPLISH SPLASH
IN ANAHEIM HOTEL WATER PARKS

If soaking up the SoCal sunshine is on your travel or staycation itinerary, check out local hotels that include a water park on their list of amenities. Hotel pools are a coveted bonus for family travel. What's even cooler, however, is a water park with slides, splash pads, and fountains that add even more fun. Plus, selecting a hotel with a water park can save on entertainment costs.

For those visiting the Disneyland Resort for multiple days, schedule a down day to let your Disneyland Feet recover (not an actual medical condition). These down days are perfect for splashing without leaving the comfort of your hotel.

Think summer is the only time to enjoy a water park? You'd be surprised to find average temperatures in the 80s through October in Anaheim.

HERE ARE SOME OPTIONS FOR HOTEL WATER PARKS

**Howard Johnson by Wyndham Anaheim
Hotel & Water Playground**
1380 S Harbor Blvd., 714-776-6120
hojoanaheim.com

Cambria Hotel & Suites
101 E Katella Ave., 855-887-7689
cambriasuitesanaheim.com

Courtyard Anaheim Theme Park Entrance
1420 S Harbor Blvd., 714-254-1442
marriott.com/en-us/hotels/
snadt-courtyard-anaheim-theme-park-entrance/overview

HAVE
A HOWLIN' GOOD TIME
AT GREAT WOLF LODGE

If you're looking for fun for your pack, Great Wolf Lodge: Anaheim/Garden Grove Resort is a must. The indoor water park resort includes multiple-story slides, lazy river, water play zone, and aquatic agility course. Reserved for hotel guests, there's plenty of space to splish and splash in the park. Don't stop the fun and grab lunch at the small snack bar inside the water park serving burgers, chicken tenders, and salads.

But there's more! The resort also includes a bowling alley, ice cream shop, arcade, and interactive entertainment in the lobby. If the memory making has worked up an appetite, check out the main restaurant with a dinner buffet. We tend to stay in the resort for meals, but there are local options outside the resort. Once you're done exploring the entertainment options, head back to your room. My children loved that the hotel room had a separate "den" space with a bunk bed just for them.

12681 Harbor Blvd., Garden Grove, 888-960-9653
greatwolf.com/southern-california/anaheim-resort

TIP

Pick up a Wolf Pass to get discounts on activities around the hotel. Another bonus: You can access the waterpark on your day of arrival and departure so you'll get even more time to splash.

TACKLE THE TRAILS
AT THE FULLERTON LOOP

When you enter the parking lot, you'll see two groups of people: dutiful community members on their way to Jury Duty or amped up adventurers about to tackle the Fullerton Loop. Behind the Fullerton Courthouse is a wooded recreation area that traverses about 11 miles of trails and pathways.

It's a popular spot for beginning and mid-range mountain bikers, and also casual hikers. Because the loop is made up of streets and trails, it can be a little confusing. For your first trek, I recommend parking at the courthouse and planning to hike or bike in and back out the same way. It's an easy hike, making it a good choice for families. Point out the horses in the back yards of some of the large family homes that line pathways to younger, possibly reluctant hikers to motivate them or plan a longer stop at Laguna Lake for a picnic. The Loop is a lovely respite tucked away in North Orange County.

Fullerton Courthouse
360 W Valley View Dr., Fullerton

BECOME A BEACH BUCCANEER
AT PIRATE'S TOWER

Pirate's Tower, or Rapunzel's Tower as it's also known, overlooks Laguna Beach, one of Orange County's beautiful beaches. The 60-foot, stone-and-concrete tower was built into the shoreside cliff in the 1920s as an enclosed staircase down to the beach and remains as a fanciful background for exploration. Keep a weather eye out for sea life in the tide pools.

Plan to go during low tide, and then park on PCH and head down Victoria Drive, where you'll find steps down to the beach. It's a bit of a trek down, but you'll likely be rewarded with smaller crowds. Once there, you'll see a circular, man-made swimming pool that's now filled with sand plus the tower itself. If you've ever spent the day dreaming about princesses locked in towers or pirates on the seven seas, this is the beach for you.

Laguna Beach
lagunabeachcity.net

CHANNEL
YOUR INNER MAVERICK
AT FLIGHTDECK

Get out your shades and practice saying, "Talk to me, Goose." At Flightdeck Air Combat Center, you can step into the cockpit of a fighter jet or Boeing 737 for a flight simulation that's 100 percent fun. You don't need any aviation experience (or cool sunglasses) to be able to fly. The experience begins with a short class. Then you're ready to take off for a 30-minute flight. When not flying, friends and family can watch all the action, making it a fun group activity or team-building exercise.

The flight simulation center is part of the Anaheim GardenWalk, a multi-story, open-air shopping and dining mall. If you're not ready to give up controls, grab lunch at FiRE + iCE Interactive Grill & Bar to keep the momentum.

400 W Disney Way, 714-937-1511
flightdeck1.com

TIP
Parking is complimentary for the first hour, but validation is available in the attached garage.

RUN AWAY
TO THE CIRCUS
AT SWINGIT TRAPEZE

Have you ever seen the acrobat of Cirque du Soleil and thought to yourself, "I could do that"? Me neither. But the truth is, we can learn aerial maneuvers at SwingIt Trapeze and possibly surprise ourselves. Customers learn to swing from a trapeze (plus other circus skills like tightrope walking) alone or part of a group. Like rock climbing or zip lining, you'll wear a line while taking to the skies to maintain high levels of safety. Get over your fears and give it a swing.

SwingIt Trapeze is now tucked in a neighborhood instead of its last location in downtown Anaheim. You'll be right at home with circus performers who are ready to share their secrets to trapeze artists of all skill levels.

900 N Maple St., 877-979-4644
swingittrapeze.net

TIP

Want to add more high-flying fun to your bucket list? Check out the Orange County Ropes Course with a group to put your skills and nerves to the test.

HIT THE TARGET
AT SAUCED BBQ & SPIRITS

Are you looking for fun that doesn't miss the mark? Try your hand at axe throwing at Sauced BBQ & Spirits. The Southern barbecue restaurant offers a full menu of "plates from the pit" to pair with bourbon and whiskey. Make sure to secure your reservation for axe throwing with a party of four or more (aged 16+) in advance so you're guaranteed to have a bullseye of a good time. Wear closed-toe shoes and take your best shot! You'll reserve an hour of axe-throwing time, and can enjoy your barbecue while throwing.

Sauced BBQ & Spirits is a great choice for game day. It's located near the Honda Center if you're attending the game, but there are tons of TVs if you're watching the game over a plate of burnt ends. If you're skipping the game to sample their sauces, enjoy the outdoor patio.

1535 W Katella Ave., Orange, 714-639-9104
saucedbbqandspirits.com

RENT A SURREY
AT IRVINE REGIONAL PARK

Irvine Regional Park, you don't look a day over 125. The wooded park offers a variety of ways to spend the day. There's a small zoo, pedal boats, playgrounds, train rides, and picnic spots. One of my favorite activities is renting a surrey for a nominal fee. If you've never ridden one, it feels like a cross between a carriage and a bicycle. There are options for your group's size, including one that seats six! Helmets are provided for no cost.

Rent a surrey and explore the bike trails to get a feel for the layout of the park before deciding what other activities you'd like to experience at the park.

Parking at the park is $3 during the week, and $5 on the weekends. Surrey rentals range from $30–$40 depending on type.

1 Irvine Park Rd., Orange, 714-973-6835
ocparks.com/irvinepark

Independence Hall

CULTURE
AND HISTORY

EXPLORE LITTLE ARABIA

Recently, Little Arabia was officially designated by the city, but the area has been a hub for the Arab-American community since the 1990s. The enclave features a collection of restaurants, bakeries, hookah lounges, religious institutions, and businesses. Travel Brookhurst Street, in between La Palma Avenue and Katella Avenue, to delight in Middle Eastern culture and cuisine. Enjoy a meal from one of the many restaurants tucked in strip malls and then snap a photo in front of the colorful "Hijabi Queens" murals.

From kabobs to shawarma, bring your appetite when exploring Little Arabia. Here is a sampling of highly rated destinations:

Sababa Falafel
11011 Brookhurst St., Garden Grove, 714-242-8977
sababafalafelshop.com

Little Arabia Lebanese Bakery & Cuisine
638 S Brookhurst St., 714-833-5760
littlearabiarestaurant.com

Brookhurst St. and La Palma Ave.
littlearabiadistrict.com

SIGN
YOUR JOHN HANCOCK
AT INDEPENDENCE HALL

Visit the birthplace of the United States just a few minutes from Anaheim, or at least a replica of it. Walter Knott of Knott's Berry Farm built a brick-by-brick replica of Philadelphia's Independence Hall outside his Buena Park theme park. Explore the history of the signing of the Declaration of Independence and Constitution with a tour around the duplicated room with artifacts, like the Liberty Bell. Can you spot the spelling error on the bell? It's also on the original!

Independence Hall is open daily (excluding Christmas Day) from 10 a.m.–4 p.m. Admission is free. You can park in the Knott's Marketplace, which offers one-hour complimentary parking, and then grab fried chicken to-go from Mrs. Knott's Chicken Dinner Restaurant.

8039 Beach Blvd., Buena Park, 714-220-5200
knotts.com

EXPLORE ANAHEIM'S HISTORY
AT FOUNDERS' PARK

Celebrate Anaheim's history at Founders' Park where you'll find two historic homes in residence: the Mother Colony House and Woelke-Stoffel House. Built in 1857, the Mother Colony House museum is the oldest remaining wood-framed building in the county. It's commonly visited by local school children who are studying local history.

The two-story, Queen Anne–style Woelke-Stoffel House plus recently constructed Pump House, Carriage House, and windmill speak to the agricultural history of the city. Visit for free the first Saturday of the month from 9 a.m.–12 p.m. to learn more about the history of the city by docents in period attire. If visiting outside of the tours, you'll be able to read informative plaques about the citrus era.

400 N West St., 714-765-6453
anaheim.net/2475/founders-park

TIP
You won't miss the impressive Moreton Bay
Fig tree, planted in 1876, which served as the
model for Disneyland's Swiss Family Robinson
Treehouse, now Adventureland's Treehouse.

IMAGINE YOURSELF
IN THE BIRTHPLACE OF IMAGINEERING

Imagination met engineering in Walt Disney's backyard barn where he maintained and controlled his 1/8th-scale train dubbed Carolwood Pacific Railroad, plus spent time relaxing and planning with friends. Walt's Barn was originally located at his home in Holmby Hills, but the "Birthplace of Imagineering" was dismantled and moved to Griffith Park in Los Angeles for preservation. Explore both rail and Disney history at the barn before exploring the rest of the park.

Getting to Griffith Park from Anaheim is approximately 30 miles, so make it a day trip to enjoy all the park has to offer including railroads, zoo, Griffith Observatory, and iconic Hollywood sign. Walt's Barn is open the third Sunday of each month from 11 a.m.–3 p.m. Admission is free.

5202 Zoo Dr., Los Angeles, 818-934-0173
carolwood.com/walts-barn

TIP

Another backyard filled with magic is known as the Castle Peak & Thunder Railroad. The Disney-loving architect homeowner opens his backyard to guests on select days to examine his handcrafted recreations of the theme park and movie scenes.

TAKE IN THE ARTS
AT MUZEO

Take in the arts at Muzeo Museum and Cultural Center in downtown Anaheim. The museum is composed of two buildings. The first part of the museum is housed in 1908 Carnegie Library, which once served as the city library, and now houses a permanent display showcasing the history of the city. It's free to visit this part of the museum center.

The main gallery is across a courtyard where you'll find community events year-round. Once in the gallery, you'll be delighted by rotating exhibits ranging from historical interest to inspiring art pieces. Train lovers will delight in the annual "Muzeo Express" exhibit during the holidays.

Visit Wednesday through Sunday from 11 a.m.–5 p.m. Adult tickets are $10 (Anaheim residents $8). After visiting the quaint museum center, stroll the area to examine the art installations like mixed media "Muzeo" in front of the library or the *Hammer Time* sculpture down Center Street.

241 S Anaheim Blvd., 714-765-6466
muzeo.org

SAY "OPA!"
AT THE OC GREEK FEST

Say "Opa!" and head to St. John's Church for a celebration of Greek culture during their annual OC Greek Fest. The festival has been an annual event since 1966, although it has shifted from a picnic to Olympics to the festival we know and love today. The cultural fair includes tours of the Greek Orthodox Church, folk dancing to live music, and a carnival kid zone, but the stars of the show are the food booths with buttery baklava, traditional gyros, and grilled souvlaki. Gobble up traditional Greek flavors, and then visit the bar to enjoy Greek wine tasting and local beer selections.

Park behind the Buena Park Walmart and hop on the free shuttle to the event. Then put on your dancing shoes for some Zorba dancing, yell "Opa!", and go back to the dessert tent for another round of kataifi.

405 N Dale St., 714-827-0181
ocgreekfest.com

WALK IN WALT'S FOOTSTEPS
IN HIS DISNEYLAND APARTMENT

If you're a historian or magic seeker, you'll want to walk in Walt Disney's footsteps in one of the exclusive tours offered by the Disneyland Resort. Currently, the theme park is offering a 90-minute tour titled "Walt's Main Street Story." It's made up of a stroll down Main Street to learn of the Marceline, Missouri, inspirations and secrets of the gateway to imagination, followed by a tour of Walt Disney's private apartment inside the park and access to the private patio.

Access to the Big Cheese's private apartment comes with a big price tag: $160 per person, aged 3 and above. But for those looking for a more intimate knowledge of Walt Disney, the price is worth skipping a few churros.

1313 Disneyland Dr., 714-781-4636
disneyland.disney.go.com/events-tours/disneyland/walts-main-street-story-tour

---

TIP
Subject to availability. Theme park ticket and reservation are also required.

PUT ON YOUR LEDERHOSEN
FOR OKTOBERFEST

Prost! Anaheim locals and guests are practically required to celebrate Oktoberfest. The city was founded by German immigrants and has grown into a craft beer destination. This October, celebrate at Old World Huntington Beach Wednesdays through Sundays with bratwurst, beers, and bands. Friday and Saturday nights are 21-plus, and on Fridays those wearing their lederhosen or dirndl get free admission.

Apply your savings to your giant pretzel fund. Note: The best giant pretzel in Anaheim is at Pym Test Kitchen in Disney California Adventure.

The biergarten welcomes guests, as do the rest of the entire Old World Village stores and shops. The evening events are popular, but check out the event calendar and make sure to pencil in at least one day to watch the weiner dog races.

7561 Center Ave., Huntington Beach, 714-895-8020
oldworldhb.com

TIP

The Phoenix Club, an Anaheim institution and another popular Oktoberfest destination, relocated to Brea in 2022 but the polka plays on. Stay tuned to see what they've got planned.

EXPLORE THE EVIDENCE
AT THE RICHARD NIXON PRESIDENTIAL LIBRARY & MUSEUM

In Yorba Linda you can visit the official birthplace of America's 37th president, Richard Nixon. His modest family home was once part of a citrus ranch, but now is a permanent feature of his official museum and library. The grounds are spectacular with a beautiful garden dedicated to the First Lady Pat Nixon and an impressive museum offering an unbiased, informative look at Nixon's life and time as president, including Watergate.

Tour his house, explore the presidential helicopter, step into a recreation of the Oval Office, pay respects at the final resting place for both President Nixon and the First Lady, and explore the permanent and touring collections.

Tickets are $25 for adults, $15 for children. The library is open from 10 a.m.–5 p.m. daily, with a special events calendar consisting of speakers, seminars, and community events like a patriotic 4th of July celebration.

18001 Yorba Linda Blvd., Yorba Linda
nixonlibrary.gov

LEARN GUITAR HISTORY
AT THE LEO FENDER GALLERY

Born on an orange grove between Anaheim and neighboring Fullerton Leo Fender revolutionized the electric guitar. The solid-body electric guitar was mass produced in his Fullerton factory. His tremendous impact on modern music is on display at the Fullerton Museum Center in a gallery bearing his name. You'll find guitars, plus information on his life and company, inside the quaint museum.

Admission to the museums is $10 for adults and $5 for children aged 5–18. After visiting, stroll Harbor Boulevard in Downtown Fullerton to enjoy antique stores and restaurants like the hippie-centric Rutabegorz where salads, soups, and sandwiches hit all the right notes. The museum courtyard is filled with music and community vendors on Thursday nights in warmer months, plus a beer garden that supports the museum.

301 N Pomona Ave., 714-519-4461
fullertonmuseum.com

TAKE A TOUR
OF ANAHEIM ART

If you're hoping to learn more about the history and people of Anaheim, look to the artists who have captured both in their work. A mosaic on what is now Chase Bank on Harbor Boulevard and Lincoln Avenue showcases the history of Anaheim, and features Polish actress Helena Modjeska. You'll also find a statue of the historic Anaheim resident in Pearson Park.

In addition to mosaics, numerous murals have been incorporated in Anaheim on public and private spaces. Be on the lookout for murals downtown and even in new apartment housing developments. Another spectacular work of public art is the sculpture garden of the JW Marriott, Anaheim Resort, attached to the Anaheim GardenWalk. Snap a few photos with your favorites around town and share on social media using #100ThingsAnaheim.

HERE ARE SOME ADDITIONAL PLACES YOU'LL FIND PUBLIC ART

JW Marriott, Anaheim Resort
Enjoy the augmented reality sculpture garden
capturing the agricultural spirit of Anaheim's roots.
1775 S Clementine St., 714-294-7800
marriott.com/en-us/hotels/snajw-jw-marriott-anaheim-resort

Muzeo
Find a mixed media creation spelling out the museum's name.
241 S Anaheim Blvd., 714-765-6466
muzeo.org

Anaheim Town Square
Upbeat murals inspire the community to grow together.
2180 E Lincoln Ave., 714-956-3411
anaheimtownsquare.com/community-art

North Net Training Center
A 9-11 wrapped mural adorns the firefighting training center.
2400 E Orangewood Ave., 714-978-7304
northnettraining.net

Little Arabia
Visit the mural collection of "Hijabi Queens."
Brookhurst St. and La Palma Ave.
littlearabiadistrict.com

Center Street Promenade
From A-benches to orange crates, there's
something unexpected throughout.
Center St. Promenade
downtownanaheim.com

City Church of Anaheim
Celebrate the people of Anaheim at this exterior mural.
Broadway and Citron St.

Love Mural
Outside the Clerk Recorder, fall in love with this mural.
222 S Harbor Blvd.

WATCH ART COME TO LIFE
AT PAGEANT OF THE MASTERS

Art comes to life in a unique presentation in Laguna Beach. The Festival of the Arts of Laguna Beach offers a summer tradition, the Pageant of the Masters. Perhaps you've seen it portrayed on *Arrested Development*. If not, the presentation features a themed collection of art pieces that are recreated by living models onstage with shocking perfection. The likeness created by the pageant actors to the original art is a unique experience for art enthusiasts of all ages. In addition to seeing the pieces come to life, the show's narrator shares information through a description of the art with the support of a full orchestra.

650 Laguna Canyon Rd., Laguna Beach, 949-494-1145
foapom.com

TIP
The Pageant of the Masters is ideal for a date night. Opt for a babysitter for children under four.

BONUS TIP

Attendees are welcome to bring food and beverages to enjoy the festival. Tickets start around $40. Bring binoculars to be able to marvel at the detail and choreography.

VISIT
LA'S HISTORIC OLVERA STREET

Did you know Anaheim has a time-traveling train? Well, not exactly time-travel, but if you climb aboard an Amtrak train at the Anaheim Station, you can go back to the 1700s to learn about El Pueblo de Los Angeles, considered the birthplace of LA. The ARTIC (Anaheim Regional Transportation Intermodal Center) is a modern hub for rail, bus, and taxi. Take the train to Union Station in Los Angeles and head across Alameda Boulevard where you'll find yourself on Olvera Street. The cultural district preserves LA's Mexican heritage. The Olvera Street marketplace consists of a historic plaza, colorful buildings, and street vendors selling food, art, and other souvenirs. Grab a meal at one of the numerous courtyard restaurants.

olvera-street.com

TIP
The ARTIC, which is conveniently located near Angel Stadium of Anaheim and the Honda Center, also offers access to AMTRAK/ Metrolink service to South Orange beaches plus northern destinations like Hollywood, Wine Country, and Santa Barbara.

BONUS TIP

Connect with a Metro Rail to visit other notable LA destinations like the Walt Disney Concert Hall or Little Tokyo.

AWAIT THE RETURN OF THE SWALLOWS
AT MISSION SAN JUAN CAPISTRANO

Considered the birthplace of Orange County and the "Jewel of the California Missions" for the chain of Spanish missions, Mission San Juan Capistrano is an important landmark for the region. The grounds have been beautifully preserved, offering a glimpse at life for all who lived at the mission. Take the audio tour at your own pace or a 90-minute guided tour, which will both take you to the remains of the Great Stone Church and other landmarks.

Every March, the mission celebrates the return of swallows migrating from Argentina, who, according to the tradition, first arrived on St. Joseph's Day. The annual migration and return of the birds has become a community highlight with live mariachi, dancing, and additional entertainment.

26801 Old Mission Rd., San Juan Capistrano, 949-234-1300
missionsjc.com

CELEBRATE UNITY
AT THE BLACK HISTORY MONTH PARADE

Gather with the community and celebrate unity during the annual Orange County Black History Month Parade, held the first Saturday of February in Anaheim. There's a full day of celebration with a morning blessing at 9 a.m., followed by the parade down Anaheim Boulevard past City Hall. You'll enjoy classic cars, community groups, and musicians making their way down the street in Orange County's sole Black History Month parade. Afterwards, enjoy the Unity Festival on Center Street Promenade at the heart of the city with community booths, vendors, live entertainment, and impactful speakers.

It's a popular event that draws thousands of attendees so give yourself plenty of time to find parking either in the Center Street Promenade parking structure or in the downtown neighborhoods.

205 W Center St. Promenade, 714-579-9966
oc-hc.org

SHOPPING
AND FASHION

GET HOPPY
AT WINDSOR HOME BREW SUPPLY

Whether you're planning your beer-cation in Anaheim or want to be the next brewery in town, you need to stop by Windsor Home Brew Supply. Everything craft brewers need to get started from yeast to equipment is in stock in their Costa Mesa and Anaheim stores. Beer making doesn't need to be intimidating, so grab an extract kit to get started without having to write your own recipes. The staff is incredibly knowledgeable and happy to share insight with their customers, plus they offer classes to get you started. If you're looking for inspiration, you'll find a thoughtfully curated selection of beer on tap, plus a bottle shop. And if beer isn't your cup of tea, consider their natural wine club.

Find Windsor Home Brew Supply conveniently located among the La Palma Beer Trail breweries.

1045 N Armando St., Ste. E, 714-666-8727
windsorhomebrewsupply.com

PICK UP PIXIE DUST
AT THE WORLD OF DISNEY

Magic is in stock in the Downtown Disney District. One place to pick up pixie dust is the World of Disney store. Shop for official Disney clothing, toys, and accessories without the need for a theme park ticket. There's even an entire wall filled with mugs!

The store was recently remodeled to add hints of magic. For example, a wall of ink pots come to life as Tinkerbell flies amongst them. Another favorite is sketches on the walls that are magically drawn by an invisible illustrator.

You can save time for more Downtown Disney exploration by utilizing the mobile checkout option on the official Disneyland app. Make sure to get your parking ticket validated with purchases over $20 from the store to save on parking fees.

1565 Disneyland Dr., 714-781-4636
disneyland.disney.go.com/shops/downtown-disney-district/world-of-disney

SHOP VINTAGE FASHION
AT RARE BY GOODWILL

Thrifty prices on hipster items are on sale at RARE by Goodwill. The nonprofit charity is known for its thrift stores, but RARE feels more like boutique consignment than your typical Goodwill. RARE in Downtown Anaheim is a collection of trendy, secondhand clothing, records, and other curated items. There are household items and furniture pieces as well.

The store itself feels like a gem! You'll find displays that feel like they belong in an Urban Outfitters–type store, like emptied out television sets serving as a light feature. There's also a book-themed wall art piece that reads, "We are anything but ordinary. We are rare."

After refreshing your wardrobe with sustainable fashion from the secondhand store, snap photos in front of the "Love" mural painted on the parking garage next door.

411 W Broadway, 714-786-6642
ocgoodwill.org

TIP

Looking for other unique thrift stores? Check out Thriftyland101 with an offering of Disney goods or Buffalo Exchange in Fullerton for more on-trend, secondhand fashion. Old Towne Orange is home to numerous antique stores as well.

ADD LUXURY TO YOUR BAG
AT SOUTH COAST PLAZA

A global destination for luxury brands, South Coast Plaza is a must-visit for fashionistas. It boasts the title of the largest shopping center on the West Coast. There are the brands you've been dreaming to wear, plus the staples to complete your closet.

Families, make sure to visit South Coast Plaza during the holidays. The displays during Lunar New Year, Easter, and Christmas are showstoppers. A beloved shopping tradition: a $2 ride on one of the shopping center's carousels.

3333 Bristol St., Costa Mesa, 714-435-2000
southcoastplaza.com

TIP
Enjoy a meal at the MICHELIN-starred contemporary French restaurant, Knife Pleat, within South Coast Plaza. Both The RANCH and Poppy & Seed in Anaheim are included among MICHELIN's guide.

GO GREEN
AT ECO NOW

Refresh your laundry detergent, soaps, and other cleaning supplies from the zero waste Eco Now shop in Downtown Anaheim. Start at home by saving jars or containers like pickle jars. Then, bring them to Eco Now to fill with home and beauty products, to be sold by weight. When the soaps or shampoos run out, you can refill your jars to save waste and costs. It's inspiring to see how many ways we can make our homes greener. Plus, the glass jars with assorted soaps make me feel like I'm living in one of my Pinterest boards.

When visiting Eco Now, you'll see a variety of items that will make green swaps easy. For example, beeswax wraps can be used in place of single-use plastics. They even have biodegradable poop bags for your pooch! Eco Now's displays makes me want to live my best life where it's Earth Day every day.

207 W Center St. Promenade, 657-201-8172
econowca.com

SAVE
AT THE OUTLETS AT ORANGE

Just a few minutes down the freeway, you'll find yourself at the Outlets at Orange. Originally "The Block," the outdoor shopping mall offers over 100 name-brand outlet and factory stores like Nordstrom Rack, Saks Fifth Avenue Off 5th, Penguin, Adidas, and more. You'll find discounted clothing and footwear, plus on-season styles. The main draw is the savings, but there's even more to explore at the mall.

You'll also find entertainment at the Outlets at Orange. There's a Dave & Buster's, Guitar Center, Lucky Strike Bowling, plus an AMC 30 movie theater.

Toting shopping bags can work up an appetite, so take advantage of the numerous eateries. There's a central hub of fast and quick casual restaurants, plus various sit-down restaurants including El Torito and Market Broiler.

20 City Blvd. W, Orange, 714-769-4001
simon.com/mall/the-outlets-at-orange

TIP

Looking for more deals? You won't be able to miss the castle-like exterior of the Citadel Outlets, located in Commerce approximately 25 miles from Anaheim. There you'll find more than 130 popular fashion and budget-forward stores.

BUILD AN EPIC CHARCUTERIE BOARD
AT CORTINA'S ITALIAN MARKET

You will not get bored filling your board. There are so many ways to build an epic charcuterie board at Cortina's Italian Market. Rows of artisan meats and cheese await you, plus a variety of Italian groceries and prepared foods. Head to the local hotspot to jump on the charcuterie trend and build an epic board to share with family and friends. Everyone's going to ask where you get your stinky cheese!

If you're like me, food shopping makes me want to skip cooking and order dinner. You're in luck at Cortina's. In addition to the market, they've got a deli and pizzeria. Order a pizza to-go or a Rocky Balboa sandwich with porchetta, provolone, broccolini, garlic chili oil, au jus, and pecorino romano.

2175 W Orange Ave., 714-535-1948
cortinasitalianfood.com/anaheim

GRAB A GIFT
AT SEED PEOPLE'S MARKET

Upstairs in the Anaheim Packing House, you'll find the sweetest little shop for unique and thoughtful gifting. SEED People's Market stocks sustainable home goods and items from small businesses, meaning you'll find something you've never seen before. I love their cookbooks and cocktail kits for birthday gifts. Don't forget the card from their wall display!

Pop in Wednesday through Sunday to shop for candles, home decor, tote bags, and other treasures. If the store isn't open during your visit, check out the wagons at the main entrance of The Packing House for small gifts like dried flowers or children's toys.

Bonus: You'll also find a small movie theater where you can check out local history on film in the corner of the SEED People's Market.

440 S Anaheim Blvd.
seedpeoplesmarket.com

SHOP FRESH
AT THE DOWNTOWN ANAHEIM FARMERS MARKET

From broccoli to blueberries, you'll find the rainbow of produce available at the Anaheim Farmers Market. Every Thursday (weather permitting) from 11 a.m.–3 p.m. the traffic circle in front of The Rinks Anaheim Ice hosts a variety of vendors. Make sure to follow their social media so you'll be aware of themed weeks. In addition to fruits and veggies, there are prepared foods to enjoy there or take home, like hummus and beef jerky. You'll find a renovated trailer with thrifted styles, booths with handmade jewelry, and businesses offering their services.

The market also hosts spots to grab lunch including Hawaiian BBQ or tacos. I typically take my produce and head down to score great two for $5 or three for $7 tacos from Cervantes Mexican Kitchen.

The smaller Farmers Market makes it easy to pop over during your lunch break to shop for fresh produce and support local businesses.

435 W Center St. Promenade
downtownanaheim.com/farmers-market

BUILD YOUR
LEGO COLLECTION
AT BRICKS AND MINIFIGS

Calling all master builders and collectors. This store's for you! Bricks and Minifigs is your destination for new, used, and hard-to-find LEGO products. You can purchase full sets or shop for assorted pieces in bulk from the privately owned store. To confirm you won't go home with any missing pieces, used sets are sold constructed for you to rebuild at home. Score a retired set or explore a new series.

One of the highlights is checking out the cases of minifigs on display. What are minifigs? They're the LEGO figures, ranging from heroes to princesses.

If you're looking to thin out your collection, Bricks and Minifigs will also sell your LEGO products, including bricks by bulk there. Sets will get you a portion of the retail price, available in cash or store credit. Book an appointment to sell your items.

1105 S Euclid, Ste. B, Fullerton
bricksandminifigsanaheim.com

TIP
Don't miss the gigantic LEGO displays at the Downtown Disney District's store.

UNEARTH A HIDDEN GEM
AT ANAHEIM GARDENWALK

The Anaheim GardenWalk is an outdoor shopping and dining center with solid entertainment offerings. It's quieter than the Downtown Disney District, and just a short walk away from the resort. It's home to many of your favorite chain restaurants like PF Chang's, CPK, and Cheesecake Factory, but you'll find many hidden gems in the small businesses. Boba and tea shops, souvenir shops, and other retail options have bloomed there.

My favorite time to visit is during their themed events when small businesses and vendors come to sell their products. I think of it like a festive Farmers Market. For example, Halloween brings Spooksieboo's Halloween Carnival with shopping, photo ops, food trucks, and spooky good fun.

400 W Disney Way, 562-695-1513
anaheimgardenwalk.com

TIP

Consider the Anaheim Gardenwalk for parking when visiting surrounding events and activities in the resort district.

FIND
THE UNCONVENTIONAL
AT THE LAB

Shop for something unconventional at The Lab Anti-Mall. The outdoor mall was designed to offer an alternative to suburban sameness, giving small businesses and cafes a home. Shop Urban Outfitters, Buffalo Exchange, and Mod Ref I Common Market for new (or new-to-you) attire. Want to feel ancient? Visit the art installation/photo opportunity tunnel filled with reflecting CDs and have to explain to your children what a compact disc is.

If you ditched the kids, check out Bootlegger's Brewery or the Ruin Bar. Coffee, doughnuts, and pizza round out The Lab.

Across the street, you'll find another untraditional shopping center, The CAMP. Like The Lab, it offers both shopping and dining, but this time with an eco spin.

2930 Bristol St., Costa Mesa, 657-232-0049
thelab.com

GRAB ANAHEIM SWAG
AT THANK YOU COFFEE

I'm a big fan of small businesses that engrain themselves in the community. It's not been long since Thank You Coffee opened their doors in Anaheim, but it quickly has become a gem for Anaheim locals for a "Boring Latte," which is anything but boring with brown sugar, cinnamon, and walnut.

In addition to the delightful menu of coffee, cream sodas, and light bites like the Avo Toast with chili threads on top, the modern and airy coffee shop has merchandise to peruse including stickers, totes, tees, and greeting cards. Check out the options featuring the Thank You Coffee mascot, plus Andy Anaheim, the city's mascot. The A-shaped mascot was a gift from the Walt Disney Company and used to boost travel to the agricultural community. Now you'll find him on city updates and throughout advertising like at Thank You Coffee.

255 N Anaheim Blvd., Unit D
thankyoucoffee.com

TIP
Looking to take your coffee to go? Enjoy the shaded A-shaped benches on Center Street Promenade.

GET DROP DEAD GORGEOUS DECOR
AT ROGER'S GARDENS

Every year, Orange County's best garden center celebrates the spooky season with a themed Halloween Boutique. The store façade transforms into something extraordinary, like a pirate ship mast or a striped *Nightmare Before Christmas* maze to mirror the theme. Inside, you'll find all the things you need to make your own home hauntingly decorated. The space is Instagram-worthy, and a fun way to get into the spirit of Halloween.

While there, you can shop for all of your garden needs, even if you don't have a green thumb. If you don't want to be green with envy, make sure to leave time to visit Farmhouse at Roger's Gardens, showcasing seasonal offerings from local producers in an alfresco farm-to-table setting.

2301 San Joaquin Hills Rd., Corona del Mar, 949-640-5800
rogersgardens.com

SCORE
AT THE SOURCE

New to the shopping scene, The Source, a multi-level, outdoor shopping mall in Buena Park, offers clothing, home decor, and accessories. Some of the big draws are the K-Pop merchandise you can score at stores like K-Place and clothing from Primrose or Princeton.

Grab some boba or coffee while you explore the entertainment offerings, including a movie theater, golf zone, and karaoke spot. The Source offers a variety of dining options, ranging from quick meals like Korean fried chicken to sit-down restaurants. A favorite for younger visitors is the cotton candy vending machine, making fantastical displays of spun sugar.

Parking is free, but learn from my mistake and note not only your parking level but which entrance opens to your parking zone.

6940 Beach Blvd., Buena Park, 714-521-8858
thesourceoc.com

BRING HOME BLOOMS
FROM VISSER'S FLORIST & GREENHOUSE

Anaheim is magic. Walt Disney knew it, and so did Bill Visser. The florist brought his flora IQ to Anaheim from Holland by way of Los Angeles where he built Orange County's largest single florist and greenhouse. Visser's Florist & Greenhouse stretches the city block with a 1960s vibe that has made it an icon in the city. Inside, you'll find large refrigerators filled with your favorite flowers with ready-to-go bouquets or stems for designing your own.

My favorite part of the florist is past the sample wedding sprays and back in the greenhouse. There you'll find houseplants and rows upon rows of succulents (the only plants I keep alive). If you're looking to gift a plant, there are numerous pots to choose from to personalize the look of your greens. If you can't make it to the florist, you can also order online or by phone.

701 W Lincoln Ave., 714-772-9900
vissersflowers.com

ACTIVITIES
BY SEASON

SPRING

Tweet about the Birds You See at Anaheim Coves, 75

Shop Fresh at the Downtown Anaheim Farmers Market, 120

Spring Over to The Flower Fields, 59

Honor the Berry That Started It All at Knott's Berry Farm, 40

Go Green at Eco Now, 115

SUMMER

Eat a Deep-Fried Oreo at the OC Fair, 43

Catch a Wave in Huntington Beach, 73

Rock Out at the House of Blues Anaheim, 44

Float Down the Lazy River at Soak City, 71

Pick Your Dinner at Tanaka Farms, 48

Shake It Up at Black Tap Craft Burgers & Beers, 34

Wipeout at the Adventure Lagoon, 69

FALL

Float On Down for the Anaheim Halloween Parade, 42

Get Drop Dead Gorgeous Decor at Roger's Gardens, 125

Enter the Fog at Knott's Scary Farm, 56

Swashbuckle Your Way to Pirate's Dinner Adventure, 49

Put On Your Lederhosen for Oktoberfest, 96

WINTER

Raise a Glass at Colony Wine Merchant, 10

Take In the Arts at Muzeo, 93

Add Luxury to Your Bag at South Coast Plaza, 114

Get on the Nice List at the Grand Californian Hotel & Spa, 58

SUGGESTED
ITINERARIES

A DAY DOWNTOWN

Start Your Day with a Salt & Butter Roll at Okayama Kobo
Cafe & Bakery, 11

Unpack New Flavors in the Anaheim Packing District, 4

Chill Out at Anaheim Ice, 64

Shop Vintage Fashion at RARE by Goodwill, 112

Meat Up at Windsor Brown's, 15

Play like Kobe at the Kobe Bryant Memorial Dream Court, 62

Take In the Arts at Muzeo, 93

DAY TRIP IDEAS

Catch a Wave in Huntington Beach, 73

Imagine Yourself in the Birthplace of Imagineering, 92

Await the Return of the Swallows at Mission
San Juan Capistrano, 106

Spring Over to The Flower Fields, 59

Visit LA's Historic Olvera Street, 104

EPIC DATE NIGHTS

Catch a Broadway Show at the Segerstrom, 47

Elevate Your Evening at The FIFTH, 8

Level Up at Arcade Mission Control, 74

Two-Step at The RANCH Saloon, 46

Unpack New Flavors in the Anaheim Packing District, 4

Rock Out at the House of Blues Anaheim, 44

Set Sail for Strong Water, 2

Craft a Great Night at Craft & Arts, 55

TOP PLACES FOR FAMILIES

Make It a Homerun Visit at Angel Stadium, 65

Maximize the Magic at the Disneyland Resort, 38

Treat Yourself at House of Chimney Cakes, 21

Have a Howlin' Good Time at Great Wolf Lodge, 78

Honor the Berry That Started It All at Knott's Berry Farm, 40

Shake It Up at Black Tap Craft Burgers & Beers, 34

Splish Splash in Anaheim Hotel Water Parks, 76

INDEX

18 Folds, 4

Adventure City, 41

Adventure Lagoon, 69

ADYA, 4

All-American Brew Works, 7

Anaheim Art, 100

Anaheim Convention Center, 45

Anaheim Coves, 75

Anaheim GardenWalk, 8, 44, 49, 82, 100, 122

Anaheim Halloween Parade, 42

Anaheim Hills Golf Course, 70

Anaheim Ice, 64, 120

Anaheim Packing House, 4, 9, 26, 30, 119

Anaheim Town Square, 101

Anaheim West Skatepark, 66

Anaheim White House, 13

Angel Stadium, 7, 53, 65

Arcade Mission Control, 74

Asylum Brewing, 7

Birrieria Guadalajara, 27

Black History Month Parade, 107

Black Tap Craft Burgers & Beers, 34

Blind Rabbit, The, 30

Brewery X, 7, 65, 68

Bricks and Minifigs, 121

Broken Timbers Brewing Company, 7

Bruery Tasting Room, The, 7

Buffalo Exchange, 113, 123

Cambria Hotel & Suites, 77

CAMP, The, 123

Center Street Promenade, 11, 101, 107, 124

Cervantes Mexican Kitchen, 26–27, 120

Chain Reaction, 44

Chance Theater, 51

Citadel Outlets, 117

City Church of Anaheim, 101

City National Grove of Anaheim, 53

Colony Wine Merchant, 10, 24

Cortina's Italian Market, 118

Courtyard Anaheim Theme Park Entrance, 77

Craft & Arts, 55

Craft by Smoke and Fire, 17

Discovery Cube, 54

Disney on Ice, 52

Disneyland Resort, 12, 18, 32, 35, 38–39, 41, 44, 58, 76, 95

Don Churro Gomez, 31

Downtown Anaheim Farmers Market, 120

Dueling Ducks Brewing Co., 7

Eco Now, 115

El Patio Drive In, 27

Farmers Park, 4, 35

FIFTH, The, 8

Flightdeck, 82

Flower Fields, The, 59

Focaccia Boi, 24

Founders' Park, 90

FRAN, 5

Fullerton Loop, 80

Georgia's Restaurant, 9

Golden Road Brewery, 65

Grand Californian Hotel & Spa, 23, 58

Great Park Balloon, 50

Great Wolf Lodge, 78

Han's Homemade Ice Cream, 19

Haunted Car Wash, 57

Healthy Junk, 4

Honda Center, 7, 52, 53, 68, 84, 104

Honey & Butter, 35

Honey Pot Meadery, 7

House of Blues Anaheim, 44

House of Chimney Cakes, 21

Howard Johnson by Wyndham Anaheim Hotel & Water
  Playground, 77

Huckleberry's, 14

Huntington Beach, 73, 96

Independence Hall, 89

Irvine Regional Park, 85

Islands Golf Center, The, 70

Italian Pizza Rosa, 25

Joe's Italian Ice, 18

K1 Speed, 72

Kip Barry's Cabaret, 49

Knott's Berry Farm, 40–41, 56, 89

Kobe Bryant Memorial Dream Court, 62

Kroft, The, 4

La Casa Garcia, 27

La Palma Beer Trail, 6, 110

Lab, The, 123

Lazy Bird, 28

Le Petit Paris, 35

LEGO, 121

LEGOLAND, 41, 59

Leo Fender Gallery, 99

Linbrook Bowl, 63

Lindo Michoacan 2, 27

Little Arabia, 88, 101

Little Arabia Lebanese Bakery & Cuisine, 88

Little Caboose Taco Shop, 26–27

Love Mural, 101, 112

MAKE Bldg., 5

Mama Cozza's, 22

Marri's Pizza, 25

Medieval Times Dinner & Tournament, 49

Mission San Juan Capistrano, 106

Monkish Brewing, 4

Muzeo, 93, 101

Napa Rose, 23

North Net Training Center, 101

Oak Canyon Nature Center, 67

OC Fair, 43

OC Greek Fest, 94

ocV!BE, 68

Oga's Cantina, 12

Okayama Kobo Cafe & Bakery, 11

Oktoberfest, 96–97

Old Towne Orange, 113

Olvera Street, 104

OMG Dessert Lounge, 35

Original Pancake House, 14

Outlets at Orange, 116

Packard Bldg., 4

Pageant of the Masters, 102

Pali Wine Co., 5

Parkestry, 8

Phantom Ales, 7

Phoenix Club, 97

Pirate's Dinner Adventure, 49

Pirate's Tower, 81

Pizza X, 25

PokiNometry, 64

Ponderosa Park, 66

Popbar, 19

Poppy & Seed, 4

Pour Vida Tortillas and Taps, 20

Puesto, 27

• •

Radiant Beer Co., 16

Ralph Brennan's Jazz Kitchen, 32

RANCH Saloon, The, 46

Randy's Donuts, 33

RARE by Goodwill, 112

Requiem Cafe, 3

Richard Nixon Presidential Library & Museum, 98

RISE Rooftop Lounge, 8

Roger's Gardens, 125

Roscoe's House of Chicken and Waffles, 9

Rosine's, 29

Ruby's Diner, 34

Sababa Falafel, 88

Salt & Straw, 19

Sauced BBQ & Spirits, 84

Scratch Room, 14

SeaWorld, 41

SEED People's Market, 119

Segerstrom, 47

Sesame Place, 41

Sidecar Doughnuts & Coffee, 33

Six Flags Magic Mountain, 41

Soak City, 71

• •

Source, The, 126

South Coast Plaza, 47, 114

Splitsville, 63

Stereo Brewing, 7

Strong Water, 2

Sugarbuzz, 19, 34

Sunbliss Cafe, 28

SwingIt Trapeze, 83

Tacos El Patron, 27

Tacos Los Cholos, 27

Tanaka Farms, 48

Thank You Coffee, 24, 124

Thriftyland101, 113

Tocumbo Ice Cream, 21

Top of the V, 8

Trader Sam's, 2

Universal Studios, 41

Unsung Brewery, 5

Urbana Anaheim, 26–27

Visser's Florist & Greenhouse, 127

Walt's Barn, 92

Walt's Main Street Story Tour, 95

Willie's Eatery, 14

• •

Windsor Brown's, 15, 24

Windsor Home Brew Supply, 110

WonderCon, 45

World of Disney, 32, 111

Zombee Donuts, 33